The Be

To Come

M. David Chambers, D.Min.

Note: The author makes no such claim that the contents of this book contain the exhaustive solutions to the matters discussed. The contents herein are designed to promote and provoke further study in God's word, as to how He desires you to live out your Christian faith, within the institution of marriage.

Cover Design: DDC 4 Him Productions
ddcproductions@earthlink.net

Inside Photos: Mickey's Creative Photography
www.mickeysphoto.com

Cover Art courtesy of Ric Horner, Electric Canvas
www.electric-canvas.com

Editors: Faye Boyd, Kathy Oakley, Lavon Perkins and Luke White.

All scripture used within this book are taken from the King James
Bible, © 1961 by the National Publishing Co.

First published by Dog Ear Publishing
4010 W. 86th Street, Ste H
Indianapolis, IN 46268
www.dogearpublishing.net

ISBN: 1-59858-006-X
Library of Congress Control Number: 2005928481

This book is printed on acid-free paper.

Printed in the United States of America

Acknowledgement of those who helped make this dream reality:

The ever-gracious Holy Spirit, whose inspiration created this work.

My dear wife Melissa and sons, Noah and Micah whose love and patience I cherish as one of my greatest treasures.

My family and extended Antioch family whose love and support are a constant source of strength and inspiration.

Dr. Bill Hines and Dr. Howard Eyrich for their inspiration and use of the "one anothers" of marriage.

Kurt Warner and the First things First Foundation for permission in using Kurt's inspiring story.

Dennis Jernigan and Shepherd's Heart Music for permission to reprint "All in All" © 1999.

This Book is dedicated to all who desire to enjoy "relationships by God's design." Though this book will approach the subject matter from the point of view of marriage the material is fail-proof for any relationship.

May His blessings fill your hearts and homes always.

Contents

Beaversovin & the Lifetime Guarantee

I am proud to offer with this little book a written lifetime guarantee. Years ago as I worked in appliance repair I quickly learned that the quality of most major appliances was decreasing about as steadily as their cost was rising. For instance, as I would go out on a job to work on a washing machine I would hope that when I walked through the door I would be looking at an older model rather than the newer, more expensive ones. The reasoning behind this seemingly strange desire was simple, in most cases the older washers were much easier to work on because there were very few parts that would go bad. I could almost diagnose the problem before I even began to take the machine apart on the "old faithfuls", but not so on the "new and improved versions". The most common failure on the older models was a $12 part called a "wig-wag" – that's right a "wig-wag"- it was a simple part that kept the washer washing and could be replaced in five minutes or less. Conversely on the newer models you would sometimes spend an hour or more just diagnosing the problem with a test meter, because there were so many electronic parts that, quite frankly, were cheap. Having said all this, let me get to my point, having this experience has caused me to truly seek and value a written guarantee on appliances, as well as most other items I purchase.

It seems though, that all such guarantees carry with them the qualifier, "limited". The guarantee I offer you is no exception. There is one thing that must take place before I will guarantee the principles in this book-**application!**

Let me expound on this idea with a simple, but true story from my childhood. When I was 10 years old my parents approached me with what seemed to be the most wonderful news I had ever received, the expectation of a little brother. Having been an only child for ten years the news of someone to play with and love was exciting. I shared this news with virtually everyone I came in contact with and 9 months later there he was, the ugliest thing I had ever seen. Now don't get me wrong my brother is much more handsome than myself at this point in our lives,

but to an eleven year old the sight of a newborn child (delivered naturally) was almost
scary. Soon thereafter though, Brett was at
home with us and we quickly bonded. As
time went on and Mom went back to work, I
had the opportunity to baby-sit my sibling
often, and for the most part everything went
smoothly when I did. Not so one fateful day
when I was watching cartoons after school,
and Brett had gone into the kitchen for his
fairly routine "cooking spree". Every so
often, he would go into the cabinet, pull out a
frying pan, place it on the stove and using a
plastic spatula, begin to "cook" something he
called "Beaversovin". What exactly is
Beaversovin? To this day I have no idea, but
he certainly enjoyed preparing it, and whenever you would ask what he was cooking
Beaversovin was your answer. Normally this
was harmless fun that we took pictures of
and loved sharing with others, but on this
particular day Brett decided to "kick it up a
notch" and actually turned the stove on. The
burner quickly heated to red hot status and
before I could get to him he raised his hand
up, spoke the word, "hot" and placed his lit-

tle hand right on the stove eye. Needless to say he received major burns on his hand that were in the same concentric circles as the heating element. To say the least, this gave us all quite a scare. You see, Brett understood that the burner was hot, yet did not apply that knowledge, resulting in injury. Now, let me just say one would not expect a 3 year old to react any differently, but the story makes a profound point - **knowledge does not equal wisdom**. Although I am thoroughly convinced the principles in this book will ensure the best is yet to come in any relationship, I also understand the reality that if they are not applied they simply will not work. It's that simple! I guarantee that if you utilize these tools from God's word the best is yet to come, if you do not then I guarantee you trouble lies ahead. So let's jump right in...by the way Brett's hand is just fine today, and he has a healthy respect for applying what he learns. My prayer is that you will too.

"My son, if thou wilt receive my words, and hide my commandments with thee; 2 So that thou incline thine ear unto wisdom, and apply thine heart to understanding;

3 Yea, if thou criest after knowledge, and liftest up thy voice for understanding; 4 If thou seekest her as silver, and searchest for her as for hid treasures; 5 Then shalt thou understand the fear of the Lord, and find the knowledge of God. 6 For the Lord giveth wisdom: out of His mouth cometh knowledge and understanding. 7 He layeth up sound wisdom for the righteous: He is a buckler to them that walk uprightly. 8 He keepeth the paths of judgment, and preserveth the way of his saints. 9 Then shalt thou understand righteousness, and judgment, and equity; yea, every good path." Proverbs 2:1-9

Introduction

Marriage is perhaps the oldest institution known to man, instituted by God himself in the Garden of Eden **(Genesis 2:18-24)**, and what a wonderful institution it is. I, for one, am so thankful that in his infinite wisdom God looked down and saw, "it was not good for man to be alone." I am also certain Adam shares this sentiment, considering his first day must have been the longest of his life since there was no Eve.(Okay, bad joke, but you get my point.) What a beautiful picture of the first father escorting his daughter to the groom we find in the union of Adam and Eve. To think that God Himself was the first one to "give away" the bride warms the innermost part of our being- or at least mine as I am a hopeless romantic. The very thought that a man and a woman are given the gift of love and a lifetime to multiply the good times as well as divide the bad, warms the heart. Thinking back on the years I have spent with my lovely bride, Melissa, I am overwhelmed with the amount of souvenirs (memories) we have collected. I am also keenly aware of the fact that it, "would not have been good for me to be alone." I have to face facts, Melissa is my better three-fourths, not better half as some would say. God has truly completed my life by "cleaving" me together with my "helpmate." Our match must have truly been one made in heaven, because no one on earth would have dreamt of such a union. If you haven't yet gotten the fact that I am extremely happy in my marriage, let me just say it, "I am daily overwhelmed with the beauty of our lives together!" There, I said it, realistically though, marriage, even at its best is not always easy. I am not in any way making the false statement that my marriage is perfect, or that it is not, often times, much like work. The fact of the matter is, marriage is a never-ending work in progress which requires diligent effort to remain successful. What if I were to tell you though, whether you have been married for 50 years or just began dating, the best still lies on the horizon for you and your spouse? I doubt there is any couple alive that would not be excited by that possibility. Well, the simple fact of the matter is...it's true. That's right, no matter what stage of the relationship or marriage you are in, there are some simple no-nonsense guide-lines that can ensure, **THE BEST IS YET TO COME!**

Chapter One

"First Things First"

On January 30, 2000, a relatively little known young man named Kurt Warner played his way into the annals of American sports history by leading the St. Louis Rams to a 23-16 victory over the Tennessee Titans in Super Bowl XXXIV, the pinnacle of western sporting events. This feat alone was impressive, but I will never forget how Kurt then went on to acquire his place in the hearts of millions worldwide, mine included. After the presentation of the coveted Lombardi trophy and other fanfare, a reporter asked Warner on international television, "First things first, tell me about the final touchdown pass…" The reply was profoundly deafening, "First things first, I want to thank my Lord and Savior up above, Thank you Jesus." Here is a man who understood completely the truth of **Matthew 6:33**, and was not afraid to let the world know it. This biblical concept of seeking God first in all things was and still is today valid for Kurt's life and everyone else's. So as we begin our journey together through the pages of this book, let's apply this same wisdom.

Before we even begin discussing ideas on marriage, love, and relationships, we must first understand the ultimate rule for the Christian life, which inevitably infiltrates the marriage life of a Christian. Although it seems too easy, something that should go without saying, it is a necessary point to be made...

"If we seek our strength, comfort, fulfillment, pleasure and identity in any person, thing or relationship rather than God we are certain to be disappointed, and rob ourselves of the full joy the Christian life has to offer."

Too often we fail in relationships and life in general because we do not fully understand this principle. We must not fall into the habit of placing unrealistic expectations on our spouses to be our primary source in life. This is our Heavenly Father's role, and one only he can fill. In a moment we will focus on the scriptures handling of this truth. First, I would like to take a short excursion into human nature and logic before we go that route. Think for a moment about how you personally respond and attempt to meet the needs of your significant other. When one pauses to reflect on such things humility is usually the result. I know that personally I could never be trusted to furnish all my wife's needs in regards to comfort, strength, sufficiency or even simple provision. Now this is not to say I do not try, or that I will ever cease my attempts to afford her all I can, but it is to say I understand the reality that I cannot be her all in all. Humans are simply not qualified for, nor do they have the discipline in and of themselves to be someone else's totality. Having dealt with pure logic, now let's delve into pure truth. This would be a great place to interject an entire manuscript on why I know that the Bible is God's word and absolute truth, but for the sake of time let me just say this: It is not only unlikely, but impossible that a book written over a 1500 year span by over 40 different authors, from every background imaginable, that is seamless in every way could be anything but Divine. Now, back to the issue at hand, that God alone is our sufficiency. Scripture echoes this truth from beginning to end as we see everyone from the great leader Moses emphatically proclaiming the source of his strength in **Exodus 15:2**, to **Jude** the dear brother of Jesus reminding those in contention for their faith of Christ, that God was their sanctification, salvation, and sufficiency in his letter, written some 1500 years later. These examples serve as mere bookends to the hundreds of such references which may be found between them. One would be hard pressed to find a single author of the canonical works who did not express this thought process in some fashion within their writings.

For simplification purposes however, let's focus for a moment on one particular verse in this line of thought, **2 Corinthians 3:5.**

"Not that we are sufficient of ourselves to think any thing as of ourselves; but our sufficiency is of God."

The jewel we uncover here is the veritable truth that Paul's faith, confidence, competence, and sufficiency were all found in the reliable unsurpassed power of Almighty God, not man, and certainly not in himself. If anyone had the right to speak on such things it must have certainly been this beloved apostle. Here was a man who had been shipwrecked, beaten, thrown to the lion's, and imprisoned for the sake of the gospel of Christ. Without a doubt here was a man who had witnessed firsthand by many infallible proofs that God was his all-in-all. I believe the lyrics to a popular praise hymn would summarize Paul's feelings on this matter very well…

All In All

You are my strength when I am weak
You are the treasure that I seek
You are my all in all
Seeking You as a precious jewel
Lord to give up, I'd be a fool,
You are my all in all
Jesus, Lamb of God, worthy is Your name
Jesus, Lamb of God, worthy is Your name
Taking my sin, my cross, my shame
Rising again, I bless Your name
You are my all in all
When I fall down, You pick me up
When I am dry, You fill my cup
You are my all in all.

May this be our heart's song as well, in life and marriage, for we need not look any further to realize that what applies to the Christian life in general must certainly apply to the specifics. If you choose to put this little book down right now, at least go away with this, God alone must be your strength, comfort, fulfillment, pleasure and identity. This is not to say that our spouses cannot be used as instruments in His hands to carry out some of the aforementioned functions, but it is to reinforce the fact that He is still, and will always be the ultimate source.

Understanding this principle, let's agree together to stop expecting divine results from our human counterparts. I reiterate, this is a position rightfully held by the Sovereign of the Universe alone. God is the only one who has made and has the power to keep any such promise of being your all-in-all.

"It is better to trust in the Lord than to put confidence in man." Psalm 118:8

"But they that wait upon the Lord shall renew their strength; they shall mount up

with wings as eagles; they shall run, and not be weary; and they shall walk, and not faint." Isaiah 40:31

"Have not I commanded thee? Be strong and of a good courage; be not afraid, neither be thou dismayed: for the Lord thy God is with thee whithersoever thou goest." Joshua 1:9

"...for He hath said, I will never leave thee, nor forsake thee." Hebrews 13:5b

Having laid the "chief cornerstone" of our study let's now continue our construction of a marriage wherein the best is yet to come.

Chapter Two

"Where the Problem Comes In"

Although I am not ready to sign on as a big Bob Dylan fan, I did run across a profound quote the singer/songwriter made some years ago that applies perfectly to the material in this phase of our journey, "A mistake is to commit a misunderstanding." If we can agree that this statement is one of truth, then we must pause here to admit we make a lot of mistakes in our marriages today, misunderstandings which are acted upon. As a result, we are witnessing one of, if not the worst period in history in regards to the breakdown of the family. Sadly, the divorce rate for Christians is reported to be as high, if not higher in some cases, than that of non-believers. One need not be a rocket scientist to understand this statistic indicates that something is wrong, badly wrong. In reality most relational problems and divorces arise from inadequate, inaccurate or just plain wrong understandings of what love and marriage are intended to be according to God's definition.

When I am doing a marriage enrichment seminar, this is the point where I ask those in attendance to take the time to briefly jot down their thoughts, understandings, and definitions of what marriage is and should be. I am of the opinion many of the responses I get are what I would call "Sunday school answers," which are what we know the answer to be, but aren't really sure we buy. For the most part, I get some really good answers though. I realize however, that when some of the answers are shared with the group by those brave souls who dare answer aloud, that their viewpoints are quite faulty. Maybe their tenets in general are close, but rarely do I get the complete definition of marriage from God's word. This truly is where the problem comes in.

For the past couple of decades especially, marriage has been strapped with unrealistic and misguided assumptions and expectations. Whenever you see a marriage in distress, or even approaching that juncture, you will find both or at least one of the two involved have an assortment of poor definitions and expectations of marriage, more impressive than the selection on the value menu at your favorite fast-food restaurant. In marriage, it seems Murphy's Law always kicks in, and you find that what you expected is not what you get, and vice versa. Where do these misconceptions and poor definitions come from exactly? The answer is multi-faceted but can normally be pinned down to at least two main sources. Culture and nurture are often the culprits in this misunderstanding game. Culture affects those who are around you as you are growing up and developing your own ideas and definitions of what love and marriage is to be. This cannot help but affect the views you carry into adulthood, and subsequently, into your relationships. Simply put, we live what we learn.

We must stop imposing our ideas and expectations on our marriages, and begin superimposing God's ideas and expectations on our marriage!

Taking all of this into account, we have adequately proven the ideas and ideals we carry into marriage will determine whether or not the union is a successful one or not. In a beautiful article I once read on the subject online (Though I could not find it again.), the author makes the sincere plea, "That we not miss out on the sterling moments of marriage because our ideals are wrong or out of sync." This synchronization alluded to must be a synchronization, or alignment with God's ideal, as well as your mates. Common sense dictates that you cannot move forward unless you are both on the same page and scriptures dictate that it must be God's page **(Ref. Proverbs 3:5-6).** Let's discuss how to accomplish this alignment.

Start your journey in this regard by talking about your expectations and ideals for marriage at length. This is not to be a five minute conversation, but rather an ongoing process of communication in which you leave the discussions with genuine understandings of your mate's expectations (More on how to effectively communicate these ideals may be found in chapter seven of this work.). Once this cumbersome, sometimes uneasy (although adventurous) task is complete, you are on your way. Next, you must take time to examine those expectations and definitions in light of the scripture, and determine where they do not line up. After discovering the incongruence between what the "us" in the marriage expects and defines, as opposed to what God expects and defines, there is a simple process to move forward. This process is what I call a "mayonnaise word", (any word over two syllables) SUPERIMPOSITION! Defined in its simplest terms, superimposition is; to overlay, to overshadow by placing something on top of.

In order to demonstrate how this easy to understand, yet hard to apply, process works, allow me to paint a word picture accompanied by an illustration of what I would do in the seminar. (See figure 1) First, imagine a script written on a dry erase board of what you and your spouse expect out of marriage, along with your own definitions of what it is supposed to be. Next, I will write the word "WE" in bold letters across the script. Finally, I will demonstrate the "superimposition fix" by taking my Bible and placing it over the script so as to completely obscure the script and the word "WE." This, my friends, is a picture of the fail proof remedy to all marriage problems, especially those of misconception and misunderstanding. You did not misread, properly applied, this fix would end all marital strife and discourse. <u>All</u>.

"The Superimposition Fix"
(Figure 1)

"Our Script"   "The Script"

As we close this chapter, let's summarize with the following statement. We must stop imposing our ideas and expectations on our marriages, and begin superimposing God's ideas and expectations on our marriage!

Having now read the first two chapters of the book, are you starting to get the feeling that I'm getting to a point yet? I certainly hope so. The point is, in most marriages, even those embarked upon by well-meaning Christian couples, the primary ingredient in God's recipe for success is left out. What is the ingredient? I'm glad you asked- God! From here let's move along into some Godly definitions and absolutes of the marriage institution, from the instruction manual He gave us- The Bible.

"All scripture is given by inspiration of God, and is profitable for doctrine, for reproof, for correction, for instruction in righteousness."
2 Timothy 3:16

Chapter Three

"Webster's is Good,
God's is Perfect"

Building upon the previous chapter, and making the a fortiori (Latin for logically indisputable) argument that we must begin superimposing God's ideals and expectations on our marriages, we must now more clearly define just what those ideals and expectations are. For our purposes we will depart from the normal methodology of seeking a definition (Webster's Dictionary), and utilize an even better source (The Bible). Before we begin allow me to make one of many disclaimers to be found within this book: *I have not included an exhaustive list within these pages of what God's definitions and absolutes for marriage are, but rather have attempted to cover the larger points in hopes that you will dig further into the scriptures for in-depth answers and detail.*

Theo Centric

First, let's continue in the thought process of God being the main ingredient for a marriage. Any successful marriage or relationship must first be what we call Theo centric. By definition, the word Theo simply means

God. Centric is a suffix defined as centered. Therefore, the term Theo centric in its base form indicates God-centered. We have covered this base quite well in the preceding chapters, but now you have the "official terminology." I would also like to paint a simple word picture for you to shore up this terminology that I use without fail in premarital counseling. Imagine if you will that you as an individual are represented by a single strand of sewing thread. Reason tells us that a single strand of thread can easily be broken in two, with little effort. Likewise, imagine now that your spouse is a single strand of thread. If I were to take these two strands of thread and twist them together, logic would tell us that the "bonded" threads would be much stronger than the single threads. I would venture to say however, that I could still break these two threads without exerting much strength, despite them being twice as strong. So let's stop there, two are certainly stronger than one. Even Solomon, whose wisdom was known the world over, agreed with this point.

"Two are better than one; because they have a good reward for their labour. *10* For if they fall, the one will lift up his fellow: but woe to him that is alone when he falleth; for he hath not another to help him up. *11* Again, if two lie together, then they have heat: but how can one be warm alone?" Ecclesiastes 4:9-11

This is where the process comes to a screeching halt for many. They understand they are stronger with a partner, but fail to realize they are still markedly weak. Now, let's imagine for arguments sake that God is a log chain. You know the kind I mean, the one that used to hang in the wood shed until it was time to hook it to a mule or tractor to drag a huge tree out of the woods. Here is where Theo centricity enters the picture; if you were to take these two strands of thread and interweave them one at a time into the links of this chain, imagine their new durability. At this point, there is no possible way that I could break either of these two threads. Not only are they impervious to the strength of my hands, but I could literally hook this chain to two separate tractors and flip one of them without breaking the threads. What we have here is a perfect picture of a Theo centric marriage- one in which the man and woman have intertwined their individual lives with God and have not simply doubled their strength, but have joined their strengths with the omnipotent strength of their Creator, a strength that none can rise against. Herein we see an earthly representation of the conclusion of the Ecclesiastical verses above, as we find that wise King of Israel, Solomon, making the claim, **"a cord of three strands is not easily broken." Ecclesiastes 4:12**

To give more credence to this point, let's look at another simple, yet profound illustration. For this illustration, simply imagine you as an individual seeking to walk daily with God as did Enoch in **Genesis 5:24**, and as we are commanded to do in **Ephesians 5:15**. A Christian seeking to unite in marriage would certainly desire an "equal yoking" **(Ref. 2 Corinthians 6:14)** and therefore, would assume that the spouse would also be walking daily towards a closeness with God. (For those who are already in an unequal yoke with an unbeliever, seek further counsel from **1 Corinthians 7:13-16**)   To complete this illustration, picture in your mind two people walking towards the same goal; they cannot help but come closer to each other. The certainty that two people walking towards closeness with God, becoming closer to each other is inevitable. One of the young ladies that I had the opportunity to offer pre-marital counseling offered this take on the matter. "One's heart should be so deeply buried in God, that the only way that their intended spouse can find them is as they become so buried themselves." This logic certainly applies even after the "search" is over and the union begins.

So there we have it, our first definition and absolute of marriage- it must be Theo centric. Now you have a "mayonnaise" word to use on your friends.

A Picture of Christ and the Church

The next ideal of Christian marriage is that it should be a picture of Christ and His bride-

the church. This essential truth is based on
the Pauline epistle of **Ephesians 5:22-31.**

" Wives, submit yourselves unto your own
husbands, as unto the Lord. 23 For the husband is the head of the wife, even as Christ
is the head of the church: and He is the Savior of the body. 24 Therefore as the church is
subject unto Christ, so let the wives be to
their own husbands in every thing. 25 Husbands, love your wives, even as Christ also
loved the church, and gave Himself for it;
26 That He might sanctify and cleanse it
with the washing of water by the word,
27 That He might present it to Himself a glo-
rious church, not having spot, or wrinkle, or
any such thing; but that it should be holy
and without blemish. 28 So ought men to
love their wives as their own bodies. He that
loveth his wife loveth himself. 29 For no
man ever yet hated his own flesh; but nour-
isheth and cherisheth it, even as the Lord
the church: 30 For we are members of His
body, of His flesh, and of His bones. 31 For
this cause shall a man leave his father and
mother, and shall be joined unto his wife,

and they two shall be one flesh. *32* This is a great mystery: but I speak concerning Christ and the church. *33* Nevertheless let every one of you in particular so love his wife even as himself; and the wife see that she reverence her husband."

Granted, one could spend an entire book just mining the gems found within this passage on the joining of two hearts and biblical expectations thereof, but for the sake of brevity, let's focus on the concept as a whole.

Within this passage, one quickly finds that God has ordained a specific hierarchy within the life of a Christian, and within marriage. Above all, a point which ties directly into what we have already been discussing is found, that God is above all. Then we find that the husband is given a higher level of responsibility in the union. Now ladies please bear with me here, if you hang in there long enough to get the true meaning of this point, I believe that you will find it to be one of comfort, instead of belittlement. Note that I did not say that he husband was given a higher level of importance, but a higher level of responsibility. There is a big difference in the two. When one considers the context of the Bible in its entirety, we find that God values every human life the same regardless of gender. When the Spirit leads the apostle Paul to pen these words, "wives submit to your husbands as unto the Lord," he has not sentenced you to a position of inferiority. Much to the contrary, the submission here, when taken in context with all that surrounds it, presents the lady as one to be revered and respected in a special way. This kind of reverence and respect is exactly what a true woman of God deserves. No less! Too long have the wires been crossed in this controversial passage. The point is the husband has a responsibility to God to be the leader in the Christian home, spiritual and otherwise. Many would have us believe that this is to take us back to the days of the proverbial caveman who ruled his wives with a club in one hand and her hair in the other. This view is erroneous and any man reading this should highlight that fact here in the book and in your own hearts and minds as well. Godly submission is a relinquishing of responsibil-

ity to one whose duty it is to take that responsibility. Although misunderstanding has led
many to believe that submission = inferiority,
the truth is, it cannot be so.   If that fallacy
were founded in truth, it would mean that
Jesus was inferior to God, as we find Him
gladly submitting to the Father.

**"But Jesus answered them, "My Father wor-
keth hitherto, and I work."** *18* **Therefore the
Jews sought the more to kill Him, because
He not only had broken the sabbath, but
said also that God was His Father, making
Himself equal with God.** *19* **Then answered
Jesus and said unto them, Verily, verily, I say
unto you, The Son can do nothing of Himself, but what he seeth the Father do: for
what things soever He doeth, these also
doeth the Son likewise.** *20* **For the Father
loveth the Son, and sheweth Him all things
that Himself doeth: and He will shew Him
greater works than these, that ye may marvel.** *21* **For as the Father raiseth up the dead,
and quickeneth them; even so the Son
quickeneth whom He will.** *22* **For the Father
judgeth no man, but hath committed all**

judgment unto the Son: 23 That all men should honour the Son, even as they honour the Father. He that honoureth not the Son honoureth not the Father which hath sent Him. 24 Verily, verily, I say unto you, he that heareth My word, and believeth on Him that sent Me, hath everlasting life, and shall not come into condemnation; but is passed from death unto life. 25 Verily, verily, I say unto you, The hour is coming, and now is, when the dead shall hear the voice of the Son of God: and they that hear shall live. 26 For as the Father hath life in Himself; so hath He given to the Son to have life in Himself; 27 And hath given Him authority to execute judgment also, because He is the Son of man. 28 Marvel not at this: for the hour is coming, in the which all that are in the graves shall hear His voice, 29 And shall come forth; they that have done good, unto the resurrection of life; and they that have done evil, unto the resurrection of damnation. 30 I can of Mine own self do nothing: as I hear, I judge: and My judgment is just; because I seek not Mine own will, but the will of the Father which hath sent Me."
John 5:17-30

Within this very passage in which we see the Lord displaying submission **(verse 30),** we find the preceding verses **(17-29)** confirming that He is equal with the Father in every way. How do the two reconcile? If he is fully God then why does he submit? The answer is simple if we remember the previous definition of Godly submission. Although an equal part of the Trinity, Jesus understood that the Father had the responsibility of directing the perfect plan of redemption, while He held the responsibility of being the earthly manifestation of said plan. No inferiority can be found here, just responsibility taken by its rightful owner.

My wife often tells other ladies that she is more than pleased with the scriptural "responsibility plan" within the home, because she finds relief in the fact that she is freed from many unnecessary worries and stress that I am responsible for.

To be certain though, there is a huge breakdown in this process when the man refuses to take his role correctly. When this is the case, the wife is then left to much prayer and meditation to discern how the Spirit would have her respond. Rest assured, He certainly will respond **(Ref. Matthew 21:22).** In this prayer, and reaction to it, be careful to test the spirits as we are cautioned to do by the apostle of love, John in his first letter, to be certain that your own spirit does not lead you awry. I would further sympathize with one in such a difficult predicament and direct them to the words of **Romans 14:1-22** which clearly display the truth that we all have to give a personal account to God for our actions, regardless of the circumstances surrounding us. In other words, a wife in this situation is not exempt from living as God dictates in his word, any more than a husband who may find himself in a similar situation. We simply do not live according to God's statutes in hopes of how our spouse will reciprocate. We do this because God says so, and because we love Him.   In this is the comfort that, although this may not make for a very comfortable situation, God will be our comfort and will reward us in the end. So to answer the question I so frequently get in this regard, "How long do I continue to put up with this aggravation?" The answer is just what you said the day you made your vows, "till death do you part." This seems especially harsh to the one enduring such hardship because the other refuses to do things God's way, but I see no scriptural exception, save infidelity. Now let me just add before I incite your innermost anger, that I am not in any way implying that anyone remain in a situation wherein their life is endangered. What I am trying to get across is that we must never give up on the one we chose to be our life's mate. One need only look at the example of Christ in this regard as He never gave up on us, despite the fact that we quite literally treated and continue to treat Him as badly as can be possible. Although there is much more to be said here, we will save that for another work, and get back to the discussion at hand.

Moving forward through this Ephesian text, we can now begin to unveil the husband's primary responsibility, to love his bride as Christ loved the church. How much was that? The answer is immeasurable and indescribable, but we do know that the love was unbounded, as displayed in its outward manifestation, his death. **John 15:13** does not imply but rather insists that there is no greater love than to lay down your life for another. That, friend, is how much Christ loved His bride, enough to give all He had, not limited to, but including His own life. This is how a husband is expected to love his wife, enough to give everything for her. Herein lies one of the real breakdowns in Christian marriages, most men are too self-centered to love to this degree. Before you tune me out men, know that I am not insinuating that I always do this either, but it is a daily goal, for I know it is a scriptural requirement. This must become your daily goal as well, if you desire to "do marriage" God's way.

We must also take the time to discuss the reasoning behind Christ taking His responsibility towards His bride correctly- that reason, redemption. Nowhere is the reasoning for Christ's entrance, life, and exit from the scene of humanity more clearly summarized than in **verses 26 and 27** of the **Ephesians** text (printed above). The word choice employed by the Spirit is magnificent in this passage as we see that Christ died to sanctify, cleanse, and then present to Himself a perfect bride without blemish.   Husbands this is your Christian duty, to communicate and strive towards the sanctifying, and cleansing of your marriage. All of this is to be done with the purpose of becoming holy as a couple. Just as Christ had a purpose in this, so must you, that you may have that special gift to present back to the one who loved you without measure. This is, according to **verse 31** (a reminder of the first marriage from **Genesis 2:24**) one of the biblically acceptable reasons for the marriage union. This truth is in stark contrast to why many join together in holy matrimony these days, which normally boils down to feelings. Here again is another book waiting to be written, but let it suffice to say that your feelings will deceive you and change like the shifting sands of the deserts. Keep in mind that the heart is the most deceptive thing known to man, and beware of its trickery as instructed in **Jeremiah 17:9** which reads, **"The heart is deceitful above all things, and desperately wicked: who can know it?"** Do not fall into the trap of trusting your own emotions and thought processes to guide you towards your life's mate. In this monumental matter, trust God alone, who is never changing.

"Trust in the Lord with all thine heart; and lean not unto thine own understanding. 6 In all thy ways acknowledge Him, and he shall direct thy paths." Proverbs 3:5-6

"Every good gift and every perfect gift is from above, and cometh down from the Father of lights, with whom is no variableness, neither shadow of turning." James 1:17

"Jesus Christ the same yesterday, and to day, and for ever." Hebrews 13:8

A Picture of the Trinity

Perhaps one of my favorite understandings of marriage in the life of a believer is found in its necessary likeness to the Holy Trinity. This picture is best understood by the use of a couple of simple graphics. (figures 3 & 4)

Figure 3

In figure 3 above, one can see a simple illustration of the Holy Trinity. Although it goes without saying that all illustrations and analogies break down at some point when trying to explain something as intricate as the Trinity, this simple triangle will serve us well for our purposes. Understanding that the triangle itself is the representation of the Trinity as a whole, we then examine that like all triangles, it has three distinct sides. Without the existence of all three equal sides, you do not have a perfect triangle, but when you do, the three combine to make one, which is an indisputable fact. This holds true with the triune God. Although He is one, there remains the fact that there are three equal parts; the Father, the Son, and the Holy Spirit. Clearly we see that God is three in responsibility and manifestation, yet in the whole, just one entity. Only to the over-analytical mind is this difficult doctrine. For anyone who believes **Genesis 1:1**, that God was able to create the heavens and the earth, this is no great feat. A God with that kind of power can exist in whatever form He desires.

Figure 4

Next we will discuss figure 4 above. In this illustration, we see that our triangle looks much the same as the Trinity triangle. There are still three distinct sides, yet as before, only one triangle. In this triangle however, we find a home in the center which represents the Christian marriage. In order for a successful Christian marriage to exist, it must have at its pinnacle the Trinity-God. Once this capstone is in place, the sides, each representing one party to the union, can be put into place. Just as the analogy of the log chain and threads, without God the whole illustration falls apart. The same will be true of the home. Just look around you and see the proof in our world today. Enough said.

Get Out and Take the Super Glue with You!

Okay, I realize that the title of the next definition on biblical marriage is a bit odd, but once we've completed this section I think you'll agree it is a very fitting title indeed. You see, get out is the first truth seen in the **Genesis 2:24** definition of marriage. "**Therefore shall a man leave his father and his mother, and shall cleave unto his wife: and they shall be one flesh.**" Perhaps one could argue that go away, or leave would be more accurate, but they are all part of the scope of what we are being told. However you choose to say it, the meaning remains the same, a separation must occur for marriage to work. With this in mind let's look at the Hebrew word used for leave in this passage to see if the original text sheds more light on the subject. The closest English likeness to the word used here is azab. Azab is defined as; to relinquish, or forsake. Aside from its definition the tense is important to note as well, that tense being the imperfect tense. What that means for those of you who like me, did much better in foreign languages than in English is simple- it is an action of relinquishing or forsaking that should have already taken place at some point. This is to say, the verse indicates that before the marriage ceremony is complete the husband, in this case, has already relinquished or forsaken someone or something. This is not to be an action that is left undone when the "I dos" are spoken. Okay, so what is he to have forsaken? In the passage we see that it speaks specifically to the leaving of father and mother, but the indication as it lines up with the whole of the passage and other scripture is that everything in his past is to be left behind. Why this would be important, would be a legitimate question for one to ask here. The purpose is to ensure that the past, and all that it carries with it, do not hinder the union of the two to be wed, so a new home and life together may be successfully forged. It only stands to reason that a husband who constantly runs to Mom and Dad, or any other past source, with his life issues and/or marital problems will never truly bond with the one he is supposed to be one with. Do not misunderstand me here, this is in no way intended to make the inference that Godly counsel from parents or others is not valid after marriage. To the contrary, we are commanded to seek Godly wisdom. The implication is, one confides in and seeks solace from his or her partner in life first. This highlights again the need for the couple to be striving for holiness, so both parties feel comfortable sharing <u>everything</u> with each other.

In order to more clearly understand the second major portion of this scripture, we will once again go to the original text. The Hebrew word for glue is dabaq. Cleave, which is the English equivalent for dabaq is what is used in our English translations, and its definition brings to mind superglue. The definition is to adhere permanently, to glue, or cement. I never cease to be amazed at God's sense of humor, and before you even think it, no, I did not just look in the mirror. I am referring to the way He always gives me personal examples to share from the pulpit, and even in my writings, to more fully explain what I am studying or trying to teach. This idea of cleaving is no exception. Just moments before I sat down to finish typing this chapter, I had taken a break to work on a clock my stepfather had given me to fix. The repair was a minor one, which required one screw and one nut being replaced, and things were going pretty well too, until I got out the superglue that is. You see I am one who wants to be sure that when I fix something that it never breaks again. This obsession with fixing something right requires a perpetual supply of two things; duct tape and superglue. For this particular application I chose the latter. All I needed to do was place one miniscule drop of this magic fluid on the screw threads so that it would never work its way out again, but something went wrong, terribly wrong. Before I knew what had happened, I realized that the screw had received the glue alright, but it was glued to me instead of the clock! If that weren't enough, I also had a pair of needle nose pliers and a paper towel attached to my hand. I suppose if there is an upside to this, it would be the fact that I now have no distinguishable fingerprints, as they are now a part of the screw, pliers and paper towel. This is little consolation though, seeing as I am not the criminal type, and cannot think of any other advantage to such a thing, but I digress. The point is simple, this is what is supposed to happen within a marriage, the husband is to leave all and be bonded together with his wife, just as if they had both been coated in superglue. The tense of the verb is quite important here as well, it is that of the perfect tense. This signifies the action has taken place at some definite point in time, but has infinite results. This bonding is to be one of such closeness and strength that it is insoluble and causes the two to become one permanently. Remember this "one flesh" principle, for it will play an important role in future discussions. A necessary point to reflect on takes us back to our other analogies and illustrations-God is the superglue, and **"what God hath joined together let no man put asunder." (Ref. Matthew 19:5-6, Mark 10:6-9)** Oh, did I forget to mention to the ladies this whole leave and cleave process certainly applies to you as well.

Before we move on to the next section, I just had to mention that the clock is working great. I just hope that screw never needs to be removed. That glue truly is a marvel – but nothing compared to God's ability to adhere two hearts together. Give it a try.

Chapter Four

"What Love Is"

"*I want to know what love is, I want you to show me...*" In 1984 the well-known band Foreigner sang these words that quickly became a teen anthem. It is no wonder this song became a crossover hit being played on radio stations with a variety of formats ranging from easy listening to hard rock. After all, isn't this one of the questions you spend the greater portion of your young life trying to answer? If you are at all like me, you looked in all the wrong places to find that answer, and kept on coming up short. The sad thing about my search was that I was shown the answer both in print and in action throughout my childhood. Between my parents, grandparents, family and extended family at my home church I should have known full well the answer and how to share it. Like many young people however, I assumed it had to be more complex than what I was being told. How could the same word that we flippantly threw around in regard to our favorite food, or song be used in regards to the intimacy of a personal relationship with someone? How do you know if it's genuine or not? These were but a few of the "issues" I had in seeking a worthwhile understanding of this powerful four letter word. In the end I am happy to say that the nurture and teachings I received led me to the very place I started in my quest for answers- the Bible.

Although this chapter is just an extension of chapter three, this final definition in our study of what we are to be superimposing over our own ideas requires so much attention, I have chosen to single it out. The complexity of love is nowhere on earth summarized and simplified more eloquently than in **1 Corinthians Chapter 13**.

"Though I speak with the tongues of men and of angels, and have not charity, I am become as sounding brass, or a tinkling cymbal. 2 And though I have the gift of prophecy, and understand all mysteries, and all knowledge; and though I have all faith, so that I could remove mountains, and have not charity, I am nothing. 3 And though I bestow all my goods to feed the poor, and though I give my body to be burned, and have not charity, it profiteth me noth-

ing.*4* Charity suffereth long, and is kind; charity envieth not; charity vaunteth not itself, is not puffed up, *5* Doth not behave itself unseemly, seeketh not her own, is not easily provoked, thinketh no evil; *6* Rejoiceth not in iniquity, but rejoiceth in the truth; *7* Beareth all things, believeth all things, hopeth all things, endureth all things.

8 Charity never faileth: but whether there be prophecies, they shall fail; whether there be tongues, they shall cease; whether there be knowledge, it shall vanish away. *9* For we know in part, and we prophesy in part. *10* But when that which is perfect is come, then that which is in part shall be done away. *11* When I was a child, I spake as a child, I understood as a child, I thought as a child: but when I became a man, I put away childish things. *12* For now we see through a glass, darkly; but then face to face: now I know in part; but then shall I know even as also I am known. *13* And now abideth faith, hope, charity, these three; but the greatest of these is charity."

This is the passage that has been embroidered, painted, recited and written for more wall hangings and marriage ceremonies than many others combined. A favorite discourse familiar to even the least discriminating bible student, this chapter touches on each facet of the heavenly gift of love. In our attempt to superimpose God's definitions and ideals over our own to achieve success in our marriages, let's take a deeper look into these poetic words penned some nineteen hundred years ago, to more clearly understand what love truly is.

First, we must clearly explain that the word charity in this passage is the English equivalent to love. More specifically, the word used in the Greek of the original text is agape. Since there are four primary words for love used in the Bible, we must fully understand the difference. First we will look at eros, this one is simple as it is where we get our English term erotic. This is a physical love that to be certain, has its place in the contents of this book, but in another discussion altogether. Next, we examine phileo. Phileo love is where the great city of "brotherly

love", Philadel-
phia gets its name,
and that's just
what it means,
brotherly love.
Now, let's look

True love is not just an emotion!

momentarily at stergos, which is a natural
affection. This is the general love we have for
members of our family, simply because they
are family. "I love you because you are my
brother."   The love used here though is a
much deeper love than either of the previous
three which brings us back to agape. Agape
love is the unconditional selfless love which
is displayed to us daily by God Himself. This
is the same type of love that successful marriages are built on.

As one begins to examine more closely the
contents of the "great love chapter" it
becomes readily apparent that this is not the
same kind of love one has towards pizza or
their favorite song on the radio. This is deep,
real deep! This kind of love is far from being
condensed as an emotion, it is an action that
is far more powerful than any emotion could
ever hope to be.

Paul immediately tells us that even if he had all the abilities known to man, and the wherewithal to use them if he did not do so in love it would be useless. He finalizes the chapter by reiterating the power and importance of true love, by saying that even faith and hope could not surpass or out last it. The point he is trying to drive home in the beginning and end of the chapter is that faith and hope will be perfectly completed in heaven, but love will be that which we participate in for all eternity.   So we get the point- love is the most powerful thing imaginable. It is the very thing that caused a perfect, holy God to look upon us thick-skulled, weak creatures with compassion and then set in motion the redemptive plan of salvation. This kind of love is not merely something that God does, it is a very part of his essence. That's powerful, any way you slice it. What a privilege to know that kind of power has been extended to us, and we can, in turn, extend it back to its original source by extending it to others. By now I hope I have you excited about what it is, so without further delay, let's define this pinnacle of powers.

In verse four we find an indication that love will not always be easy. I am satisfied that you have already said enough amens to fill your quota for several Sundays after that statement. We all know love is not always fun and games. Again I must make the point, true love is not just an emotion, or sweet feeling. As we recall how God displayed this agape love towards mankind, we remember that it culminated in the greatest suffering ever known to man, the crucifixion. The very term excruciating, signifying great suffering and pain, comes from the compound word "ex-crucis", meaning out of the cross. All the suffering we may endure in our lives while on this ball of dirt will never compare to that experienced by Christ on the cross as He defined love. Understanding this we must go into love and remain therein knowing that if God Himself experienced suffering in the name of love we will too.

On a different line of thought within verse four we find that love is kind. What a novel idea, that we be kind to each other in marriage. One would think this could be left out of a book about marriage. The logic would tell us that two hearts desiring to leave everything behind and be joined as one would already know that they are supposed to be kind to one another. **(Ref. Ephesians 4:32)** Sadly, this is not the case. Who on earth would not be kind to themselves? Apparently many of us since married couples are now one flesh and stay the course of not being kind to their other half. With the risk of sounding cynical, I must say that the couples that I most often deal with either don't get this, or they don't show it. Either way, if they are to experience the joy of real love much work needs to be done, because this is not a suggestion for genuine love it is a command. That is one of the beauties of every principle found within this book, no matter where you are in this regard it's not too late to try things God's way.

Next up in verse four we begin to uncover a very timely truth in regards to love in our "me society" of the 21st century. This truth seems on the surface to be another "no-brainer" that we all should understand and employ, but I fear we have a long ways to go. The words read, **"love envieth not."** What exactly is envy anyway? In its base form,

envy is discontent over another's success. If
this is the definition, how on earth could a
spouse justify envy towards their own mate?
The very thought of such a thing is absurd
when we go back to the "one flesh" principle
we have discussed at length. We need to be
as ecstatic over the accomplishments of our
husband/wife as we are our own, because
that is just what they are-our own.

As we close out our dissection of verse
four we are left to discuss the facts that, **"love
vaunteth not itself, and is not puffed up."**
This is not to say as one individual described
to me that, "Love doesn't stuff itself and
become fat." That was a direct quote, believe
it or not. What these two terms mean collectively is that one displaying true love does
not become unduly proud in themselves.
Anything we manage to succeed in is a joint
effort with our spouse, and further we must
remember that as a Christian anything of
worth we accomplish is not of ourselves, but
of the LORD. Arrogance has no place within
the Christian home.

Verse five of **1 Corinthians 13** continues
the defining process of love by attacking

unseemly behavior. This point could not be more cut and dry, therefore, I will be brief in its expansion. Simply stated, true love acts out the principles of **Philippians 4:8-9**, which reads as such;

" Finally, brethren, whatsoever things are true, whatsoever things are honest, whatsoever things are just, whatsoever things are pure, whatsoever things are lovely, whatsoever things are of good report; if there be any virtue, and if there be any praise, think on these things. 9 Those things, which ye have both learned, and received, and heard, and seen in me, do: and the God of peace shall be with you."

If you find yourself in a quandary as to whether something is unseemly behavior or not, just take a moment to hold it up to this "seemly behavior litmus test."

Once done with correct marital behavior, Paul moves on to the monster called selfishness. It is imperative that we remember the definition of agape at this point. Agape is unconditional love, one more interested in the well-being of the other than self. This principle is difficult however in a world that tells you that you must always look out for number one. This is an issue we will deal with more in chapter 5 so for now let's focus on selfishness itself. Selfishness within the marriage union undermines the basic "one flesh" premise of marriage, to say nothing of its scriptural incorrectness. According to these words, love is not love unless it is in constant observance of the Romans 15 principles of seeking the good of another above your own. It seems that whenever I share this unchanging truth with anyone I always get the same response, "if I am always looking to take care of the needs of someone else, then what about my needs?" My response is always the same as well, I simply smile and say, "Think about it-if both parties in a relationship are truly acting this out, everyone's needs are met, and after all which is more fun; meeting your own needs or letting someone else."

Seeing that four major aspects of love have been packed into verse five, let's now move to the fourth. This portion indicates that love is not easily provoked, but you would not know it if you were a fly on the wall in many "Christian homes" today. The reality is that it takes very little to "light the fuse" of our human anger, especially in our homes. I struggle with this on a regular basis, as I am a typical Type A personality. I look at the world through eyes of logic in most cases and when my lovely bride does the slightest thing out of sync with my own perception of that logic, I admittedly enter into a spiritual struggle. Everything in my mind tells me that I need to swiftly and pointedly "get her straight." This, however, is not in keeping with the definition of true love, or the scriptural understanding that, "the wrath of man worketh not the righteousness of God," from James 1:20. It is upon this realization (Thanks to the Holy Spirit.) that I immediately have to make the effort to "take these wrongful thoughts captive" in order to act out my love for Melissa correctly, utilizing the "seemly" behavior aforementioned in this discussion **(Ref. 2 Corinthians 10:5)**. Needless to say, I am not always successful and have to move on to the apology stage often, but this is the pattern, this is true love, this is my goal.

As we finalize the power-packed lineup of love virtues in verse five, we end with the "thinketh no evil" spiel. This too, is a point that speaks for itself but deserves our attention. Here it is in a nicely wrapped package for you, "true love gives the benefit of the doubt." That is to say, if you truly love someone you will work under the assumption that they mean well, until you know beyond doubt they have ill-intentions. Typically when we act or react to something in regards to our spouse we truly do have good intentions, but remember we have come from two different backgrounds and our thought processes may be on different levels at times, so this virtue of love is crucial. If we do not act out this virtue in our homes, we are in for many unnecessary disagreements, and needless stress. Easily said, not so easily done, but if you promise to pray for me in this regard, I promise to do the same for you.

Verse six of our passage points out the simple fact that a Christian never rejoices in those things which are against God, but in those things which are pleasing to Him. This, in fact, is the only instance where we are taught that anger is acceptable, that being towards sin. This is in perfect compliance with our previous point that holiness should be the goal in the home. If this is the goal then sin should be discouraged at every juncture, and holiness contended for as if our marriages were at stake, because they are.

Paul's use of defining terms is wrapped up within my favorite section of this passage, verse seven. Within these words we are told that true love bears, believes, hopes, and endures all things. What a mouthful. Now I understand that this is saying love puts up with, and remains hopeful in all things, but I need some clarification here. I, for one, need to know what is meant by "all things" when I read this scripture, so let's see what we can find in this regard. The word *all* here can be translated back into the Greek as pas. Pas is defined as such; each, every, any, all, the whole, everything, some of all types. This is the same word used in the well-known passage of John 3:16, which indicates that *all* who believe in Him will not perish, but live eternally. So does this mean that true love puts up with, remains hopeful in and endures everything? I see no way around it. Further, I need to know for how long love does this. Again, we will go to the Greek for enlightenment. The Greek equivalent to endure in English is hupomeno, which means to endure or bear bravely and calmly ill treatments. In its usage here there appears to be no end to the action. This would fall perfectly in line with the way Christ, our perfect example of true love, reacted towards us.

"But God commendeth his love toward us, in that, while we were yet sinners, Christ died for us." Romans 5:8

So there we have it, God's definition of love. In contrast to the definition found in *Webster's New World Dictionary* for love which says, strong affection, we see the true understanding that, "Webster's definitions are good, but God's are perfect."

Chapter Five

"The Showstoppers"

At this point in our journey you should be quite proud of yourself. Proud because you care enough about your marriage to have just spent a great deal of your already precious time reading over 7,000 words in the past two chapters in order to get a better understanding of what God meant love and marriage to be. I would caution you not to get too carried away though, since pride will be dealt with in just a few moments as we list it as one of the top two "showstoppers" in regards to effective biblical marriage.

I will never forget working with a church choir many years ago on a Christmas musical called *Celebrate*. The choir was relatively small and on a tight budget, so we had asked the choir director at a neighboring church for permission to use some of his music to perform this cantata. For weeks we worked on the songs, and although we were hitting the right notes at the right time something was missing. Since I couldn't put my finger on what the problem was, I began to pray. In my prayer time I felt the Spirit leading me to simply ask the choir members what they thought. At the next practice session, that's just what I did. I began by telling them how well they were doing and that I appreciated all their efforts but felt like something was missing, and I desired their input.

At first I got that "deer in the headlights" stare one often gets to questions encouraging heartfelt response. Finally, the preacher's wife spoke up and said, "For some reason I am just not comfortable with the program." After much discussion and numerous others echoing her sentiments, it seemed as if we all had a burden lifted off our backs. The problem was that simple. Even though we were doing what we believed to be the right things, at the right times, the missing factor was heart. The Spirit was saying to many of us in the background that this just wasn't right.

Now I have to admit that this all worked out for the very best, as we put together a moving tribute to our King by utilizing many beautiful Christmas carols to tell the story of his birth. Although this change was undoubtedly the right thing to do, (thank you "Mrs. Preacher") to say the least it was a showstopper. With only two weeks before

Christmas, here we were with nothing prepared, so we had to take a step back, pray and adjust our plans according to the Spirit's prompting.

Many times in our marriages a similar thing happens. We are going about our daily lives the best we know how, and even trying to superimpose God's ideal over our own, but something's just not quite right. The marriage is not fulfilling, and we don't know what the specific problem is. When this occurs, we must take a step back, pray, examine then adjust our plan. In regards to our marriages, however, we can usually blame one of two main perpetrators, which we will label "showstoppers." Their specific names are Culture and Self. I must caution you that these are not the only two possibilities, rather they are the most common and destructive. If we could truly get a handle on these two, I am of the persuasion that many other pitfalls would fade into the background, as most others are simply symptoms of these two greater problems. Understanding that marriage is a spiritual institution, we must also accept the fact that Satan hates it and is daily seeking how he can use one of these showstoppers on us. With this in mind, we must work diligently to identify the enemy's strategy and thwart his efforts at every turn. Therefore, I will borrow the words of the late great D.L. Moody, "to the work."

Culture

Let's begin our study on the enemy's attacks by examining more closely the showstopper called culture. In and of itself, culture is not necessarily bad. The right kind and amount of culture can be a wonderful teacher, but only when it is rooted in the supreme moral code of our Creator. Today's culture is far from being rooted at all, much less in a Supreme moral code. In fact, culture today seems more of a fluid principle than an absolute. What we are being fed today sounds especially intelligent on the surface but in reality is quite foolish. What I am referring to is "moral relativism", the erroneous belief that there is no absolute truth, and mankind is free to do whatever is right in his own eyes. This type of thinking sounds alarmingly like the world the young preacher Timothy was warned about in the year 67 A.D. chronicled in **2 Timothy 4:3 and 4.**

3 For the time will come when they will not endure sound doctrine; but after their own lusts shall they heap to themselves teachers, having itching ears; 4 And they shall turn away their ears from the truth, and shall be turned unto fables.

The condition of today's world also bears a striking resemblance to the Nation of Israel's endless cycle of problems recorded in the book of **Judges**. They too, were doing what they thought was right in their own eyes. What a horrific life this would be if everyone bought into this idea of moral relativism - we would literally be living in a state of anarchy. The absence of absolute truths, and definite moral code would pave the way for "anything." Think about how our world would be if everything were acceptable. Although this is a scary thought, this seems to be the direction we are heading, but we must not be lulled into such erroneous doctrine unawares. Culture such as this is not only self-destructive in the end, it also destroys marriages in the meantime. Within this kind of culture we are inundated with false views of what is acceptable. Once again, we must go to the only reliable source of truth we have at our disposal.   You guessed it - the Bible.

A primary example of a faulty view culture holds is that on divorce. Culture would have you believe that you may as well go ahead and get married even if you are uncertain, and then if the union does not work out, simply go online and file your own "no - fault divorce."   What a misnomer! How could there be any such thing as a no - fault divorce? This belief however, is what culture teaches through television sitcoms, talk shows, popular music, magazines, and virtually every other form of medium imaginable. Society tells us that we can wipe away a marriage union as easily as we wipe tears from our cheeks, and that no trace remains. I have one word for this kind of thinking that culture is trying to force feed us, "Garbage."

With each couple who asks me to perform their marriage ceremony, I make the same statement without compromise, "Divorce is not an option for a Christian who says 'I do!'" How can you make such a claim? You might ask. How can I not make such a claim? I will answer. In the words of the old preacher from **1 Corinthians 9:16, "…woe be unto me if I not preach the gospel."** You see, unlike some preachers who agree to perform any wedding that they are requested to do, I care enough about those for whom I am acting as a joining agent to tell them the truth. I refuse to join them if they will not hear, or at least profess to believe it.

Not only is culture a little off in its view of divorce, it's dead wrong. A dear Filipino couple in our church family often tells a fitting story in this regard. The dear lady says that when she and her husband were wed she told him, "This marriage is final. No exchanges and no returns!" They understood the institution correctly, and have fifty-one wonderful years to show for it. Marriage is a sacred institution that is intended to be insoluble (Remember the crazy glue.), not a childish game wherein you get unlimited "do -overs." We know this to be truth from the unbending words found in **Malachi 2:16, "For the LORD, the God of Israel, saith that he hateth putting away (divorce)."** How much plainer could He have been? So if you are in a tough spot in your marriage, don't give up. Keep trying to do things God's way and life in the home will improve. Certainly this only finds complete success when both individuals are actively working to live His way. I am convinced, however, He will reward your personal obedience to him and shunning of worldly views on this matter.

I have to pause for a moment here to address those who have already been down the rocky road of divorce. Let me comfort you with these words: God is more interested in where you are going than where you have been. In other words, let the mistakes of the past stay where they belong as you move forward in your walk with Him. Mistakes and sins of the past are to become milestones of education in the life of a believer, and not a dead end. Do not ever forget that God's grace was, is and always will be sufficient to move us beyond any sin or painful experience. This holds true whether this sin was committed by, or against us. Most of the people I meet who have experienced this hateful tool of the devil have a difficult time truly moving forward, even though they will tell anyone who asks, they have. To those who have these feelings because you were part of a divorce, take time to be comforted and moved by these words:

"Remember ye not the former things, neither consider the things of old. *19* Behold, I will do a new thing..." Isaiah 43:18-19

"And He said unto me, My grace is sufficient for thee: for My strength is made perfect in weakness. Most gladly therefore will I rather glory in my infirmities, that the power of Christ may rest upon me." 2 Corinthians 12:9

"And he that sat upon the throne said, Behold, I make all things new. And he said unto me, Write: for these words are true and faithful." Revelation 21:5

If divorce were the only place that culture's thinking missed the mark, I would gladly stop here and move on to the second of the greater showstoppers, but this is not the case. Below is a set of jokes I came across on the internet while doing research for a seminar.

HAPPINESS
To be happy with a man, you must understand him a lot and love him a little. To be happy with a woman, you must love her a lot and not try to understand her at all.

LONGEVITY
Married men live longer than single men, but married men are a lot more willing to die.

MEMORY
Any married man should forget his mistakes, there's no use in two people remembering the same thing.

APPEARANCE
Men wake up as good-looking as they went to bed.
Women somehow deteriorate during the night.

PROPENSITY TO CHANGE
A woman marries a man expecting he will change, but he doesn't.

A man marries a woman expecting that she won't change, and she does.

DISCUSSION TECHNIQUE
A woman has the last word in any argument. Anything a man says after that is the beginning of a new argument.

COMPREHENSION
There are 2 times when a man doesn't understand a woman - before marriage and after marriage.

Please understand that I am no prude, nor am I a radical who cannot take a joke. I have to admit that these are just plain funny, but I certainly take them for what they are- jokes. However, I am afraid that to many in our culture these kinds of thoughts are more than humorous, they are reality. This kind of false reality demeans the institution of marriage, an institution sanctioned by God. We must acknowledge the fact that (when held up the light of truth,) culture's thinking comes up miserably short more often than not. When we give thought to this jaded reality, there is always the tendency to feel overwhelmed in a sense of futility, but this need not be so. Although culture is drastically left of God's standard, we ourselves do not have to be.

As believers we are instructed to be "in the world and not of it." I will concede doing so is not easy because the world's ways look awfully good sometimes, but we have to remember that we are just passing through to something much better as we stay the course of God. This requires us to be radically different **(ref. 1 Peter 2:9)**, transformed **(ref. Romans 12:2)**, and even hated by the world **(ref. John 15:18-21)**. I have yet to find anyone who claimed they wanted the world to hate them, for this very idea is contrary to one of the most basic human needs, to be accepted. Even if this thought process seems contrary to that which seems so important to us, I see no allowance for compromise. It's either God's way or the world's, not both.

You see God fully expects to look down into the world and see the believer, but he does not expect to look into the believer and see the world. Since God left no room for "fence walkers," we must choose, and when we choose correctly, the world will hate us. **"...know ye not that the friendship of the world is enmity with God? Whosoever therefore will be a friend of the world is the enemy of God." James 4:4b** Join with me in avoiding this showstopper called culture. Choose the right way, God's way. Make this choice in life and in marriage.

Self

Our next exposure of the enemy's plan deals with one of the most ruthless enemies of Christian marriage. This powerful foe is the enemy within and is hard to overcome because we have a great affinity for him. His name is self. That's right, in many cases we are our own worst enemy in life and most certainly in marriage. More specifically we will deal with the bane of humanity called pride - the metamorphosis of healthy self-esteem into unhealthy self-importance. It is vital to good mental health that one has enough self worth to realize they are God's most cherished treasure, but when self-worth crosses the line to self-important arrogance a fall is soon to follow. In this destructive process, Christ-like humility is not factored in **(ref. Proverbs 16:18).** Many of the writings found in the books of wisdom warn that pride breeds a plethora of show stopping attributes: evil, shame, disagreements, destruction, and ignorance - just to name a few.

"The fear of the LORD is to hate evil: pride, and arrogancy, and the evil way, and the froward mouth, do I hate." Proverbs 8:13

"When pride cometh, then cometh shame: but with the lowly is wisdom." Proverbs 11:2

"Only by pride cometh contention: but with the well advised is wisdom." Proverbs 13:10

"Pride goeth before destruction and an haughty spirit before a fall." Proverbs 16:18

As if these scripture weren't enough, **Romans 8:7-8** as well as, **Jeremiah 17:9,** tell us we have tainted hearts that are ready at a moment's notice to deceive us.

"Because the carnal mind is enmity against God: for it is not subject to the law of God, neither indeed can be. *8* So then they that are in the flesh cannot please God." Romans 8:7-8

"The heart is deceitful above all things, and desperately wicked: who can know it?" Jeremiah 17:9

Don't get depressed on me here, for there is hope. To illustrate this hope, I cannot help but to share with you a story of my five year old son. Noah is an only child, although my wife and I are expecting our second child even as I finish this book. Being an only child requires great imagination and skill to keep from falling into boredom. Noah has mastered this skill and rarely finds himself with noting to do. On one occasion, however, I could tell that he had succumbed to loneliness to the point of having an argument with himself. I suppose he felt this necessary seeing that his mother and I were too busy to entertain him at the moment. I overheard him in his room telling someone that they had better stop being mean to him immediately. Discerning that there was an unusual seriousness to his tone and knowing that his mom was the only other person in the house, I quickly went to scold him for being disrespectful. When I reached the top of the stairs, I saw that Melissa was in our bedroom and nowhere near Noah. After making this observation, I decide to peek in on him through the crack in the door to see just what was transpiring. What I saw was hilarious. There stood a five year old boy hitting himself in the head over and over. Before the thought even begins to settle in your mind, I must say that my son was not "losing it," just acting out his imagination. I quickly intervened as if someone else was hurting him and asked, "Noah why in the world are you hitting yourself?" Noah coolly replied, "Noah wouldn't behave himself so I had to take care of it."

We have all heard that there is much wisdom to be found in "the mouth of babes," and this incident is proof-positive. Although I am not promoting self battery in the physical sense here, I am promoting self discipline. When we come to the realization that we are not being successful in our marriage because we simply are not behaving according to God's plan, we must take action. Since pride and self are such formidable opponents our course of action must be drastic and constant. To clarify let me say that our actions should be drastic in the sense that we are determined to do whatever it takes, and with daily consistency. What will it take? This is the question at hand. For Noah, it was a little physical persuasion. For us, it must be spiritual persuasion. The fact is, we are not strong enough within ourselves to defeat the showstopper of self, but we do have at our disposal the tool that can help us. The tool I am referring to is the very Spirit of God. We must discipline ourselves on a regular basis to plead with the Spirit for his help in this regard. This is the methodology employed by "the man after God's own heart," King David. We know this to be true because his pleas for the Spirit's help are recorded in the Psalms.

"Let not the foot of pride come against me, and let not the hand of the wicked remove me." Psalm 36:11

"Create in me a clean heart, O God; and renew a right spirit within me." Psalm 51:10

For most people this principle of praying to defeat self seems a little counterproductive, but for the discerning believer, bringing in heavenly reinforcement is the only way. We must also go back to a truth from our previous discussion and be reminded that culture views most things incorrectly, including this principle of self-discipline. In our country today self-discipline is defined as; having a diet drink with a mega-sized value meal. I am not knocking diet drink aficionados, just the erroneous thought process that keeps most well-meaning people from having any discipline at all. At running the risk of sounding like an athletic shoe commercial, let me just close this point with the words, "Just do it." Make yourself act on the principles of God, as they pertain to marriage. Self-discipline is a Godly virtue **(Ref. 1 Peter 4:7)**.

Before we exit this chapter, let me add one small piece of advice. Take care to eliminate the "cultural garbage" you take into your mind and heart. If you fail to get rid of this trash, it will make the above battles more difficult. A true Christian is bound by duty to know scripture well enough to recognize when what he/she sees, or hears is incompatible with truth. When that same Christian becomes aware of such incompatibilities, he/she must have the discipline to stop the source of such things before they are programmed into their thought processes. It is a scriptural matter of guarding the heart, for out of the heart flow our actions.

"23 Keep thy heart with all diligence; for out of it are the issues of life. 24 Put away from thee a froward "mouth, and perverse lips put far from thee. 25 Let thine eyes look right on, and let thine eyelids look straight before thee. 26 Ponder the path of thy feet, and let all thy ways be established. 27 Turn

not to the right hand nor to the left: remove thy foot from evil. Proverbs 4:23-27

Don't be a victim of the "showstoppers" of culture and self.   Guard your heart, and discipline yourselves to pray them away.

"Oh be careful little eyes what you see...Oh be careful little ears what you hear..."

Scriptural References to Culture & Pride for Further Study

Culture's view vs. God's
Deuteronomy 24:1-4
Matthew 5:31-32
Matthew 19:8-9
Mark 8:31-38
Luke 16:18
2 Corinthians 6:14-18

God hates Pride
Proverbs 16:5

Pride causes us to point out other's faults, while ignoring our own
Genesis 3:11-13
Matthew 7:1-5

How to get self out of the way
James 1:5

Self-control necessary
Romans 6:12

Walk God's path not our own
1 Chronicles 13:1-14
Romans 13:13

**"Swallow all the pride you can,
it's not fattening!"**

Chapter Six

"Crabby Apples"

"Talking is sharing, but listening is caring." What a profound quote, one that is timeless and indisputable. Talking is truly a gift as we have the ability to open our minds and hearts to those around us, and share what they contain. Likewise, listening is an equally important gift because this is our chance to show those exercising the first gift, the contents of their hearts and minds are important to us as well. Over the next few chapters we will spend a fair amount of time discussing several major issues on which it is crucial for healthy relationships to have common ground. Communication will be the first, and lengthiest. There is no mistake in this placement, or length. Communication is one of, if not the most important tool you can use in your marriage to ensure the best always lay ahead. Without proper communication, you cannot begin to hope for success in any endeavor, especially in relationships. You simply cannot hope to enjoy the bounteous joy that marriage and its "one flesh" principle offer unless you know your "other half" intimately. This knowledge comes only through communication.

Without proper communication,

you cannot begin to hope for success

in any endeavor.

In regards to good communication I am "realistically optimistic." This is to say that I know that good communication is not the norm in most marriages, but I am optimistic that this can change. For our time together in this portion of the book, we will focus on the "do nots" of communication which cause us to be "crabby apples."

Even a small child understands the importance of good communication, as they begin to develop their own relationships early in life. To a child there is very little pretense, or ulterior motive to the way they communicate, they just open up and say what's on their mind. At times I enjoy conversations with children in my ministry more so than with adults, for this very reason. Let's face it, kids are brutally honest, and although this <u>must</u> be balanced with tact in our marriages, this is a great quality of good communication.

Too often, I am left to decipher and sift through what is being said in order to get to the real meaning, before I can even hope to minister to people. This problem arises in many cases because the showstoppers rear their ugly heads and have people believing that they should not share their true feelings with anyone. Although this belief has come to be an expected norm in ministerial circles, we must not allow such to become the expected norm in our homes. In order for marriage to be successful, there must be a healthy balance of sharing and caring; talking and listening.

The greatest portion of my counseling time by far, is time spent with couples in distress. It usually happens as such: a wife calls me and says, "My marriage needs some help. Could I come talk with you?" My answer of course is, "Yes, but in order for counseling to be effective, it is important that both parties come together." Here is where the difficult part enters the picture because I usually get this response, "My husband doesn't want to talk in front of someone else about our problems." "Really," I say and then proceed to ask, "Does he like to talk about it with you at home then?"   The answer is typically a resounding "No."   I wish I thought that the caller was just being negative, but experience has taught me differently.   Something about "our wiring" as men makes us think that displaying emotion and true feelings to our mates, or anyone else for that matter, makes us weak and vulnerable.   How far from Biblical truth could we be fellows?   As Christian men we must somehow (Refer to the previous Chapter.) overcome this lunacy fed to us by our culture, if our marriages are to succeed.   We must also defeat our own pride in this regard.

I don't recall anyone calling King David, one of the greatest warriors of ancient history, a wimp when he wept publicly.   What about the numerous times we find him weeping over sin and openly sharing his heart with his people? **(ref. 1 & 2 Samuel)** Furthermore, I can assure you no one thought him less of a man for how eloquently he shared his heart with the entire known world by penning his innermost thoughts in the **Psalms**.   If David is not proof enough, consider the mighty king, Solomon.   Have you read **Song of Solomon** lately?   Good grief, this book is dripping with sweet romance, but I would venture that no one questioned his manhood either. Finally I would point to all of you "he-men" that Jesus himself was never afraid to share his heart or emotions, whether that meant a word or a tear.

"And Jesus came and touched them, and said, Arise, and be not afraid." Matthew 17:7

"So Jesus had compassion on them, and touched their eyes: and immediately their eyes received sight, and they followed Him." Matthew 20:34

"And Jesus, moved with compassion, put forth His hand, and touched him, and saith unto him, I will; be thou clean." Mark 1:41

"Jesus wept." John 11:35

The above verses are but a few of the hundreds which validate my claim that Jesus communicated his heart and emotions well.

Did this make him any less powerful, or respected? I am not about to be the one who questions the power and authority of Almighty God and hope you won't either. As we venture on, the point is this: husbands, do not get caught up in the false view that being a man requires you be horrible at communication.

I'll bet you ladies thought you were off the hook on this one, huh? Although I picked on my brethren specifically since I too have battled this "meat headed" thought process, I also know that there are women who are engaged in similar struggles. Knowing this to be truth, I encourage you to examine your own willingness to share your <u>true</u> feelings with your spouse as well.

Since we have amply laid the foundation that good communication is a critical element of the marriage, where do we go from here? How about a huge disclaimer?

Disclaimer: *Although we will discuss several of the larger points of good communication, I have not even begun to skim the surface of all that effective communication entails. This portion of the* *book is intended for the sole purpose of getting you started on the right track to good communication and in no way represents the end all of communication helps.*

I guess it would be fair to field the question of why I didn't deal with all aspects of good communication within this work instead of writing a disclaimer. The answer is simple - the entirety of this book (and all that grace the shelves of my personal library) would not be sufficient space to do so. Literally, thousands of books have been written on this subject alone, so I have attempted to identify from many of those books, (though primarily the Bible) what the major helps are to get you off and running. So let's go.

Notice that up to this point I have referred to *good* communication no less than five times. I point this fact out to help you grasp the truth that all communication is <u>not</u> *good* communication. Since you have taken the time to read this book, I assume that you agree that the institution of marriage is worthy of the best you can give. Therefore, our goal is good communication as opposed to communication. What's the difference, you may ask?   The answer is simple. Yelling, derogatory remarks, frigid body language, and even physical abuse could be considered communication, but you would be hard pressed to find anyone to agree that those constituted *good* communication.   So let's depart from our introduction and dig right into the kinds of communication expected from a Christian. (Although the following discussions deal specifically with marriage, the suggestions contained within the next two chapters most certainly apply in any and every situation)

First, we will discuss two major hindrances to good communication - improper procedure and dishonesty.

Improper Procedure

Improper procedure is a politically correct way of saying that you have chosen the wrong words or methodology for the task at hand. Too often within the confines of our homes we live out the old cliché, "You hurt the ones you love the most." Where does it say that we have to live by such an absurd auspice? This goes right along with our earlier discussion that we must separate ourselves from the world and live as a sanctified group of believers, set apart to avoid unseemly behavior. I truly believe that most normal people understand that they are not supposed to speak to and act harshly with their husbands/wives, but somehow continue to practice this detrimental vice. I want to give you a short list of things to beware of in your communication in an effort to identify the enemy with the goal of defeating it:

Provocation/Harsh Words - To stir someone to an emotional response, utilizing poor word choice.

Small Talk/Excessive- The age old tactics of "clamming up", or its complete opposite of talking too much.

Incorrect Tone - The emphasis and way something is said.

Poor Timing – Saying or acting out something without regard to timing.

Malicious Body Language- The use of body motion or lack thereof to indicate unspoken emotion.

Let's take a look at these communication killers a bit more at length. In dealing with provocation we must take a moment to think of how wrong this truly is. The very thought that we would make a concerted effort to antagonize our partners in life to the point of anger is unthinkable and counterproductive to successful marriage. When we remember they are literally a part of us in the one flesh principle, we should feel awfully childish to realize we would push ourselves to rash reaction. Let's take a look at several verses from the holy writ that shed more light on how wrong provocation and harsh words really are.

"Burning lips and a wicked heart are like a potsherd covered with silver dross." Proverbs 26:23

"And the tongue is a fire, a world of iniquity: so is the tongue among our members, that it defileth the whole body, and setteth on fire the course of nature; and it is set on fire of hell." James 3:6

"A soft answer turneth away wrath: but grievous words stir up anger. The tongue of the wise useth knowledge aright." Proverbs 15:1 & 2

"He that is slow to wrath is of great understanding: but he that is hasty of spirit exalteth folly." Proverbs 14:29

"Put them in mind to be subject to principalities and powers, to obey magistrates, to be ready to every good work, 2 To speak evil of no man, to be no brawlers, but gentle, shewing all meekness unto all men. 3 For we ourselves also were sometimes foolish, disobedient, deceived, serving divers lusts and pleasures, living in malice and envy, hateful, and hating one another. 4 But after that the kindness and love of God our Savior toward man appeared." Titus 3:1-4

"With all lowliness and meekness, with longsuffering, forbearing one another in love" Ephesians 4:2

"Be ye therefore followers of God, as dear children." Ephesians 5:1

Now let's see what we can harvest from the scripture references above. The tongue, along with burning lips is a powerful set of instruments that can foster immense hurt when used incorrectly, but on the other hand, great tools of healing if used as God intended. I think that is a fair enough transliteration don't you? I would venture to say, I really didn't need to point these facts out to you, as you have inevitably experienced them for yourself. Show me an individual who makes the claim that he/she has never hurt, or been hurt, by harsh words of provocation and I will show you a prime example of dishonesty. We have all been bewildered, disenfranchised and just plain hurt by the mighty power of the tongue. The sad thing about the misuse of words is that words cannot simply be taken back once spoken. There is no way to extract the pungent smell of a word misspoken from the air in which it was spoken. This highlights the fact that we must be those who are living what we know as shown in the last five references above. We must display

Godly wisdom, restraint, patience and compassion by avoiding all word choices that stir up strife within the hearts of our mates. How exactly one goes about this, is another story altogether. I will simply refer to our discussion on how to be in the world and not of it in our previous chapter. Within the context of that discussion, we learned that a lot of prayer and discipline are necessary to achieve this difficult goal. I can assure you though that if you ask anything according to His will, He promises to hear and answer.

"And this is the confidence that we have in Him, that, if we ask any thing according to His will, He heareth us: And if we know that He hears us, whatsoever we ask, we know that we have the petitions that we desired of Him." 1 John 5:14 & 15

Having read those words, we know for certainty that God wants to help us deal appropriately with our spouses, and if we ask for and accept His help, then He is clearly ready to answer us. Please make note that we must first accept the help, then proceed to discipline ourselves to react to this help.

In case you need a "bottom line" for this section here it is: Remember that your spouse is a human with the same feelings and emotions that you possess, and anything that would hurt or provoke your significant other should be left unsaid. Choose your words carefully to stop the unnecessary fractures in your home.

Next, we will look briefly at small talk and excessive talk. Although I (based on personal experience only) think that there is a certain gender more apt to participate in the small talk arena, I will not make the stereotype. I can, however, speak of what my wife and I experienced in our home early in our marriage. My wife had absolutely mastered the art of small talk and silence. By her very nature, she is non-confrontational. This, coupled with her desire to do things God's way caused her to instantly lock her lips as tightly as the vault doors on Fort Knox at the first glimmer of an argument. You men out there who are saying, "What is he complaining about?" should be ashamed! It is no picnic when you cannot get to the bottom of an important issue due to the fact that someone will not talk, or only makes small talk. It took me the better portion of a year to finally get my wife to understand the importance of good communication, and that small talk was a communication killer. She knew full well the why of good communication, but not the how. I don't have to worry about that anymore, now I cannot get her to stop once she starts. Okay that was a joke, but things are much better because she now sees the release and freedom found in open communication.

On the other side of the spectrum is the great aggravator called excessive talk. Whew, it's getting hot in here now! This is another of the communication killers that I fear belongs primarily to a particular gender, (again based solely on personal experience, you may find the opposite to be true) but don't worry men; I won't mention that I think it's us. What I will mention is what I am certain of. This is the area, where I, personally, had to invest time and effort to achieve better communication. If what is said about the one who talks most usually being wrong is true, then I guess I have been wrong much more often than right. I still battle self with the improper thought that I need to get the last word, and plenty in between. Something inside me wants to persuade my wife by impeccable logic that I am right, and I mistakenly feel that a lot of repetition is required to accomplish this. (As I read this to my wife, she is beginning to grin like the Cheshire cat. I expect her to break out into amens at any moment.) Granted, repetition is the key to learning, but in the case of communication, can easily be overdone. So for those of you who share this vice with me, just say what you mean in the proper way and "let it go."

For our final stop in "Crabby Apples," we will wrap the final three communication killers of our list into one simple point. Not only is your choice of words important, but also the way and time in which you present them. If I were to copyright the phrase I use more often than all others in marriage counseling, I would be a rich man. That simple caution is this, "Even the right word spoken in the wrong way or at the wrong time is the wrong word." This premise is another that we have all experienced, and been guilty of. You know exactly what I mean here. Quite frequently, we are injured by the words of a mate because of the way they are said or by the body language that accompanies it. We have already discussed in the definition of true love, and will discuss further in future pages, that we are to always to give the benefit of the doubt, but this is a difficult task. When the love of our life walks up and makes a statement that we know to be truth, but says it in a hateful, hurtful or even sarcastic tone, we are prepared to give them everything but the benefit of the doubt. This is where the pieces of this "best is yet to come puzzle" clearly work together. In these situations we must make every effort to assume they mean no harm, offer a soft answer, and pray that all begins to smooth out. This is also to remind us, we are not to use hurtful tones within our conversations because they lead to provocation and harsh words.

Without belaboring the point too much, let's add the fact that we must take great thought and consideration as to the timing of a conversation, or choice of words. A prime example would be bringing up how badly you want to go to the basketball game, race, or mall alone when you've just had a discussion with your spouse about the need of spending more quality time with the family. Keep in mind the simple fact that timing truly is everything. The following verse, which my wife did in needlepoint for me hangs above my desk -

"To every thing there is a season, and a time to every purpose under the heaven." Ecclesiastes 3:1

Dishonesty

I have to admit that I feel a bit foolish even mentioning dishonesty in the context of this book, for no one alive who claims Christianity at all needs to be told that dishonesty is wrong, right? I wish! I have honestly been taken aback by the many people who have openly told me that they only tell their spouses what they need to know and in the way they see fit. They make no apologies that they are happy to rearrange the facts in order to keep the peace, and to withhold whatever secrets they deem necessary. There is one word for these tactics, lying. Regardless of whether the reasoning is keeping the peace, personal gain or making oneself look better in the eyes of another, dishonesty has no place in the Christian life, much less in the Christian marriage. The plethora of scriptural teachings on the importance of truth is so vast (Well over 300 and that's just because I stopped counting.) as to be impossible to even begin to list them all, but I have, for arguments sake, listed some primary verses below.

"Thou shalt not bear false witness." Exodus 20:16

"These six things doth the Lord hate: yea, seven are an abomination unto Him: 17 A proud look, a lying tongue, and hands that shed innocent blood, 18 An heart that deviseth wicked imaginations, feet that be swift in running to mischief, 19 A false witness that speaketh lies, and he that soweth discord among brethren." Proverbs 6:16-19

"Lying lips are abomination to the Lord: but they that deal truly are His delight. " Proverbs 12:2

"And let none of you imagine evil in your hearts against his neighbor;   and love no false oath: for all these are things that I hate, saith the Lord." Zechariah 8:17

"Be renewed in the spirit of your mind; 24 And that ye put on the new man, which after God is created in righteousness and true holiness. "Wherefore putting away lying, speak every man truth with his neighbor: for we are members one of another." Ephesians 4:4:23-25

For the sake of you dear ladies who are still waiting for your husband to follow through on old promises, let me quickly add here that false promises are not allowed either. Ladies and gentlemen, if you make a promise, keep it. Anything less is just another form of dishonesty. I know you are saying that I don't understand how busy you get, but I have no sympathy. I'll trade calendars with you in a minute! This is your spouse we are talking about. Honesty is a must. **(ref. Matthew 5:37)** If we continue to "hold hands with the world" and its thought process that honesty is optional, we will further erode the already weakened foundations of scriptural marriage. I for one do not wish to participate in such a heinous act, and I know you don't either. Pray <u>earnestly</u> for help with these communication killers, so we can throw out the "crabby apples."

"And let us consider one another to provoke unto love and to good works." Hebrews 10:24

Chapter Seven

"Salty Dogs"

It's the heat of battle in the kitchen; the husband and wife have been squared off for what seems like eternity in an exchange of poorly chosen words accompanied by hurtful tones, excessive talk, and malicious body language. The opponents are exasperated and struggle to think of the next piece of ammunition to hurl at the other. Finally it happens, the inevitable, the husband blurts it out, "Just tell me what you want to hear and I'll gladly say it!"

How many times we have heard this ridiculous phrase from the mouths of one or the other in an argument that arose from completely ignoring the "do nots" of good communication. Maybe somewhere deep in the recesses of the mind of the person that made the statement there is some sincerity, but all too often it is just another example of improper use of the gift of communication. I can honestly say, however, that I would love for someone to offer me the right words to say and the right way to say them in any discussion. I'll bet you share this sentiment. If you do, I have great news for you. Someone

<u>has</u> given us a perfect script for discussions within our marriages and otherwise. That's right, I am about to give all of you who have ever made the above statement just what you asked for, a script that will always work. If you have been paying attention at all to this point, you know that I am referring to the guidelines God laid out for us in His word.

Here again, I cannot begin to offer you all there is to find in this regard, nor do I make any kind of foolish promise that every word you are to ever speak is to be found here. The claim that I will make is that in the next page or so of this work I will give you enough of the framework of proper communication for you to build into strong Christian conversations.

Let's sketch out this aforementioned framework by discussing two major points. First we will look at exhortational speech, followed by edifying speech. Just as we mentioned in regards to the wrongful patterns of good communication, the following tips are not suggestions, but mandates in the Christian life.

Exhortational Speech

The first mandate is that we must speak to our spouses in a manner that exhorts. Exhort is just a fancy word for encourage. When one seeks the complete happiness marriage offers, they must spend time honing their skill of encouragement. I have yet to meet anyone who does not appreciate or even thrive on encouraging words to keep them motivated. Think for a moment of how much pleasure encouragement brings you as an individual to receive, and how much fun it is when you do this for others. Without further substantiation, let's look to the script I promised.

" That ye put off concerning the former conversation the old man, which is corrupt according to the deceitful lusts; 23 And be renewed in the spirit of your mind; 24 And that ye put on the new man, which after God is created in righteousness and true holiness. 25 Wherefore putting away lying, speak every man truth with his neighbour: for we are members one of another. 26 Be ye angry, and sin not: let not the sun go down upon your wrath: 27 Neither give place to the devil. 28 Let him that stole steal no more: but rather let him labor, working with his hands the thing which is good, that he may have to give to him that needeth. 29 Let no corrupt communication proceed out of your mouth, but <u>that which is good to the use of edifying, that it may minister grace unto the hearers.</u> 30 And grieve not the Holy Spirit of God, whereby ye are sealed unto the day of redemption. 31 Let all bitterness, and wrath, and anger, and clamor, and evil speaking, be put away from you, with all malice: 32 And be ye kind one to another, tenderhearted, forgiving one another, even as God for Christ's sake hath forgiven you." Ephesians 4:22-32

Well that about covers the entire communication realm we have been discussing, so I cannot encourage you enough to read this often, maybe even memorize it , it will come in handy. Specifically though, let's look at the words which are underscored. This is what we are going for; words that encourage and minister to the hearer, in this case our partners in life. In this context minister can be defined as giving help to someone selflessly. What a great standard to use for your script, if what we are about to say does not offer help to someone selflessly, bite your tongue.

Edifying Speech

Let's look at another lesser known passage for more on the correct script.

"Let your speech be <u>always</u> with grace, seasoned with salt, that ye may know how ye ought to answer every man." Colossians 4:6

I absolutely love this passage because within those twenty-one short words, is an abundance of wisdom regarding good communication. Let me show you what I mean.

This is a lesson entitled, "Salty Dogs" I shared with a group of thirty-two teenagers several years ago at a summer camp. I began by giving each of them a small packet of salt, like the ones found in your local fast food restaurants. I then proceeded to tell them that's what their conversation should always be like as Christians. Of course I got the,

"What on earth are you talking about" look that teens are masters at.   This is what I wanted, their attention.   Then we began do discuss how our speech should always be "salty", to which they began to quickly respond.   One particularly colorful young man asked," You mean rough and burning?" There is an example of how open and brutally honest young people can be, but I had to respond in the negative.   This was not what I meant at all, quite the opposite is true in fact. As a Christian our speech should always be doing the four primary things that salt does. First, salt is very effective as a preservative. I can remember as a child in rural North Carolina, how the neighborhood would get together at my Grandfather's to kill and process pigs, usually on a chilly Saturday morning. Once all the "dirty work" was done and everyone had gone home, my Mema (Grandmother) would take the hams and completely coat them in layers of salt in a huge box, where they would remain for a month or more. After the salting period was done, the hams could then be hung in the smokehouse for later use. The amazing thing about this process is that the hams could hang there for what seemed eternity and still be delicious when used. As far back as we have recorded history man has used salt as a preservative in similar fashion, due to the lack of refrigeration. How do we apply this to our speech though, is the next question. Simple, our words in life and in our homes should always be those which preserve the truth and those things found within the Philippians 4:8 guidelines.

"Finally, brethren, whatsoever things are true, whatsoever things are honest, whatsoever things are just, whatsoever things are pure, whatsoever things are lovely, whatsoever things are of good report; if there be any virtue, and if there be any praise, think on these things."

Although the words above say to think on these things, common sensibility tells us we should also be speaking these things.

Second, salt has an amazing ability to purify. Many ancient cultures used salt as a type of cleansing agent on wounds after battle, in order to cut down on the chance of infection. This would certainly not be a comfortable cleansing, but true purification never is. We have all heard the expression "throwing salt into the wound," which indicates something has been done to increase the pain. This adage may be true in regards to more discomfort, but the end result is warranted in many cases. This end result is purification, and again preservation. Although there is some controversy over whether or not this is true, it is said the cliché about salt in the wound finds its roots in the salt mines of Patmos. Patmos was the island to which John the Apostle was banished for his faith. This was the infamous island on which John penned the apocalyptic book of Revelation. While on this island John would be subjected to tortuous work in the salt mines. The prisoners would be forced to pick away at the salt deposits for long hours with rudimentary tools, or their hands. In this process it is only reasonable to make the assumption their hands and arms were scratched and injured often. Think about this for a moment, open wounds and salt deposits do not make for a comfortable mixture. Even at the end of the work day the brine water of the sea was their sink, in which they washed their hands. Uncomfortable maybe, but many believe that it was this "salt in the wounds" that kept the captives alive and more impervious to infection. Now, back to how this relates to our speech. Our speech should be that which is attempting to achieve the goal set forth in Chapter 3, of purifying and cleansing the home. If your conversation does not communicate Holiness, then it is likely a waste of words and time **(Ref. 1 Peter 4:11)**.

Thirdly, in reference to salt's four primary functions, we will look at fertilization. You did not misunderstand, salt has been used for centuries as a type of growth stimulant. Even today many fertilization agents contain salt or its by products in their formulation. So what can we do in our speech to help "grow something?" We can apply the wisdom of **Ephesians 4:29**.

"Let no corrupt communication proceed out of your mouth, but that which is good to the

use of <u>edifying,</u> **that it may minister grace unto the hearers."**

This verse speaks clearly for itself, but let me clarify. Edify means to build up. If the communication that proceeds from your mouth tears down, you have missed the mark, and are drifting into "crabby apple territory".

Finally, we must speak of salt's wonderful ability to season. This is one function of salt Americans don't need to be schooled on. It is because of this attribute that many in our nation today battle chronic hypertension. High blood pressure is a difficult force to be reckoned with because we lack the discipline required to use this "flavor enhancer" in moderation. The good news is there is no such moderation required in the seasoning of our speech. Not only are you allowed to use "salty speech" in excess, but are encouraged to do just that **(Ref. Colossians 4:6)**. Whenever and however you have the opportunity to enhance the lives of your spouse and others by your words, do so without hesitation.

There you have it, over one thousand words on how to obtain more effective communication in the home from just one simple verse. We have unequivocally proven in the past two chapters, that *good* communication is crucial for a healthy relationship. So, put this book down for a bit and go practice. Spend quality time openly, and honestly, sharing and caring with your spouse, using the guidelines above. If you do this, the results will be amazing as you watch your relationship grow to unexpected heights. Be encouraged as well, this will become very addictive and contagious. Do not forget however, if you desire to achieve these goals, proper procedure and honesty must be in place. God commands it, your spouse deserves it. Have fun, and don't let all the time you spent in these chapters be wasted, get out there and become, "Salty Dogs"!

Scriptural References to Communication for Further Study

Proverbs 14:29

Proverbs 15:1-9

Proverbs 19:11

Matthew 7:1-12

Matthew 18:15-22
John 17:21-23
Romans 12:17-21
Ephesians 4:26-32
Philippians 2:12-18
Colossians 3:1-17
James 1:1-20
James 3:1-18

Chapter Eight

"The 'S' Word"

You knew it had to happen, there was no way someone could write a legitimate book on the subject of marriage without talking about the "s" word. Since you are reading a book on the lifelong commitment of marriage, I plan to move ahead under the assumption, that you are a discerning adult, who will appreciate a straightforward approach. The taboo surrounding sexual intimacy in many Christian circles has greatly hampered acceptable views of the beauty of sex within its proper context. It seems that anytime this subject comes up it is surrounded by snickers, bad jokes, and a wealth of other poor communication techniques. I have also become keenly aware the very tone of a person's voice will change when sex is brought into a conversation. I firmly believe this type of improper handling of a God-given gift has caused many of the problems we collectively face today. Therefore, I will write candidly in my handling of sexual matters from God's perspective.

The general ideas held in regards to sex are, to say the least, varied. Everyone you come in contact with will have different views on the matter if they will even talk with you about it long enough to share their views. Sadly, this seems to be true of most Christians as well. How is it, that one of the most beautiful expressions of love between a husband and wife is reduced to a slang term? Why are people so afraid to handle this "hot potato"?   We have already divulged the answer to these questions, in the statement above. Everyone has different opinions, and are afraid that they are incorrect, so they joke about it, or avoid the subject altogether. With this mind, we will employ the same approach to sex as we did to marriage in general in our opening discussions. We first, identified the fact that many people have wrong expectations and definitions for marriage. Next, we worked to effectively find God's definitions and superimpose them over those which did not line up.   Let's do the same with sexual misconceptions.

I cannot help but mention a story shared with a large group of Pastor's at a conference I attended some years ago. The speaker was working with the college and career group at his church, and had an appointment with a young man who had just become engaged. As the excited groom-to-be entered the office he made a bee-line to the speaker's desk. Propping on the desk with a sheepish grin on his face, he proceeded to ask the following. "Professor, can you tell me what it's like to be married and have sex every single night?" The professor leaned over the desk and replied, "I have no idea, and neither will you!" What a great story to make a point. We need a better understanding of God's views on the matter. The young man meant no harm, but I am certain he learned very quickly, his preconceived notions were wrong. Many of us are guilty of the same.

As a tangent, I must mention that we are, to some extent, victims in this situation. The first of the showstoppers, Culture, has completely warped our thinking on physical intimacy. Twenty-five years ago, television networks would not even show a married couple in bed together. Media today has no such concern. When we turn our televisions on today, not only have we come to expect married couples in bed together performing the "act of marriage," but we are quite likely to see many couples in this scenario who are not married. These unwed couples are often young people, who are portrayed to be normal kids, "experimenting with nature." This experimentation theory has led many to believe that "kicking the tires, before you buy the car" is status quo. This thinking is but one, of the endless fallacies that culture feeds us about sex. In defeating this particular problem in regards to sexual understanding, I would refer you back to chapter five. You will, once again, find scriptural helps in overcoming cultures misguided doctrine within those pages.

To get back to the body of our discussion, let's move forward by simply examining a few of society's views, in a side by side comparison to God's. When you are done reading through the table, take time to consider how you, as an individual, will superimpose the right column over the left.

Society says ...	God says ...
Sex before marriage acceptable	Sex is acceptable only after "I do". **1 Corinthians 6:18-20, 1 Corinthians 7:2-36, 1 Thessalonians 4:3-8**
Sex with any partner of choice acceptable	Sex is acceptable only between man and wife. **Exodus 20, Leviticus 18, Romans 1:26-28,1 Corinthians 7:2-36, Hebrews 13:4**
Sex primarily for self gratification	Sex within marriage serves dual purpose. Reproduction & <u>Mutual</u> Pleasure/Intimacy. **Genesis 1:28, 1 Corinthians 13:5**
Fantasy's about sex harmless	Lust is a sin, and leads to emotional/mental adultery, immoral actions. **Matthew 5:27-28, Mark 7:20-23**
Abstinence absurd	Abstinence required unless married. **1 Corinthians 6:18-20, 1 Corinthians 7:2-36, 1 Thessalonians 4:3-8, Hebrews 13:4**
Casual sex harmless	No such thing exists. **Genesis 1:28,1 Corinthians 7:2-36, Hebrews 13:4**
Sex is "leveraging tool" in marriage	Sex not to be withheld in the marriage bed without reason. **1 Corinthians 7:4-5**

I must say those are some hard thoughts to handle if looked at through the blurred vision of society. Hard as they may be though, we must face facts. Thoughts from the left column led to the fall of one of the greatest civilizations known to man, Rome. I am disheartened to say, it is leading to the demise of our own as well. Improper views of the purpose and use of sex, have led to a vast array of; sexually transmitted diseases, unwanted pregnancies, and broken homes. Certainly, we could spend a great deal of time discussing the controversial points above, but due to the fact that scripture speaks so clearly for itself in this regard, we will let them do just that. After prayer and meditation, you be the judge, better yet, let God.

Although that was certainly the condensed version, the point is clear, culture has once again missed the mark. Perhaps you are one who is guilty of some of the infractions above, and are feeling pretty guilty at this point. Let me pause momentarily to remind you of the previously mentioned grace of God. *"God is more interested in where you are going than where you have been."* Again, I urge you to let the sins of the past stay there. Move forward in your walk with God. Mistakes and sins should be used as educators and motivators, to avoid future mistakes. Do not ever forget, God's grace is and always will be sufficient to move us past any sin. Many who have been a party to past sexual sin find it difficult to forgive themselves. As a result, much time is wasted confessing and asking forgiveness redundantly for the same offenses. This action is detrimental in the life of a believer, as it indicates lack of faith in the following passages;

"As far as the east is from the west, so far hath He removed our transgressions from us." Psalm 103:12

"And He said unto me, My grace is sufficient for thee: for My strength is made perfect in weakness. Most gladly therefore will I rather glory in my infirmities, that the power of Christ may rest upon me." 2 Corinthians 12:9

You see dear brother/sister, when you constantly go to God asking forgiveness of

> *Sex is the most beautiful*
>
> *expression of love*
>
> *between a husband and wife.*

the same sin, you are only reminding Him of what had already been forgotten. If you will turn from your sinful ways, God is faithful to restore you. This, He promised to an entire sinful nation and its individuals some 2,400 years ago. This, He extends to you today. Move forward in the victory found in repentance, showered with grace.

"If My people, which are called by My name, shall humble themselves, and pray, and seek my face, and turn from their wicked ways; then will I hear from heaven, and will forgive their sin, and heal their land." 2 Chronicles 7:14

Another problem facing the physical aspect of many marriages today is a lack of intimacy. The most common definition of intimacy is; as personally close as possible. Think about this for a moment. To be certain, this is as close as two humans can possibly be. Too often, couples fail to savor the beauty of guilt-free, divinely-ordained togetherness. When intercourse exists within God's parameters, it becomes the outward display of the "one flesh" principle He instituted in the Garden of Eden. It is, without dispute, a thing of beauty. Do not rob the union of this beauty via; insensitivity, or haste. Be ever mindful that coitus is not merely an action; it is an act, the act of love.

One would hope, after our lengthy handling of *good* communication, that its importance in this realm would be a given. In case it is not, let me articulate it now. As we mentioned in passing above, the lack of healthy discussion about sex is a major problem. Not only is frank discussion acceptable in marriage, it is essential. If you never communicate openly about your preferences and desires, you cannot reasonably expect them to be met. From experience, I know many of you reading this book are thinking it is too late to begin these "frank discussions". Without sounding too critical, let me say this, "Hogwash!" It's only too late if you are not willing.   Take time to pray for the right words, the right way, and the right time to speak honestly with your spouse. When you sense the Spirit's guidance, move forward to the discussion stage.   Finally, enjoy the results!

After dealing with some of the problems related to healthy marital sex, and how to move past them, let's end on a positive note. Properly handled, sex is a powerful tool in displaying Christian love. This being said, I encourage you to employ the same guidelines in your marriage bed, as discussed in chapter four, with respect to Christian love. That is to say, selflessly. One preacher was quoted as saying, "before I enter the bedroom to have relations with my wife, I pray that I will give her great pleasure." Though you may find this strange, this is selfless love. God will answer this kind of prayer if offered by a genuine heart. As foreign as this may sound, remember the definition of Agape love, it seeks the benefit of its recipient. In practicing this art, do not fear that your own needs will not be met. Anything done by God's standards, with proper motive, will be blessed. Yes, even the "s" word.

Read, and then meditate on these words of wisdom, offered by King Solomon to his son. Herein, you will find a great summarization of God's thoughts on many sexual issues.

"My son, attend unto my wisdom, and bow thine ear to my understanding: 2 That thou mayest regard discretion, and that thy lips may keep knowledge. 3 For the lips of a strange woman drop as an honeycomb, and her mouth is smoother than oil: 4 But her end is bitter as wormwood, sharp as a twoedged sword. 5 Her feet go down to death; her steps take hold on hell. 6 Lest thou shouldest ponder the path of life, her ways are moveable, that thou canst not know them. 7 Hear me now therefore, O ye children, and depart not from the words of my mouth. 8 Remove thy way far from her, and come not nigh the door of her house: 9 Lest thou give thine honour unto others, and thy years unto the cruel: 10 Lest strangers be filled with thy wealth; and thy labours be in the house of a stranger; 11 And thou mourn at the last, when thy flesh and thy body are consumed, 12 And say, How have I hated instruction, and my heart despised reproof; 13 And have not obeyed the voice of my teachers, nor inclined mine ear to them that instructed me! 14 I was almost in all evil in the midst of the congregation and assembly. 15 Drink waters out of thine own cistern, and running waters out of thine own well. 16 Let thy fountains be dispersed abroad, and rivers of waters in the streets. 17 Let them be only thine own, and not strangers' with thee. 18 Let thy fountain be blessed: and rejoice with the wife of thy youth. 19 Let her be as the loving hind and pleasant roe; let her breasts satisfy thee at all times; and be thou ravished always with her love. 20 And why wilt thou, my son, be ravished with a strange woman, and embrace the bosom of a stranger? 21 For the ways of man are before the eyes of the Lord, and he pondereth all his goings." Proverbs 5: 1 - 21

Chapter Nine

"Put Your Money
Where Your Mouth I$"

For the benefit of those who are younger than I, the title of this chapter was a popular catch phrase of the seventies. This phrase was born out of the script for a mouthwash commercial. Now that you know where the phrase comes from, let's jump right into our discussion on the all important matter of mouthwash. Sorry, I can never resist the chance to create a smile. Seriously though, we will quickly touch on what I perceive to be another pothole in the road to success in Christian marriage. That's right, this chapter is going to be, "all about the Benjamin's." For those of you older than I, let me also give you the courtesy of translation. "All about the Benjamin's," is a current catch phrase referring to the almighty dollar. You know; jack, cheddar, ducks, bills, green, bling, etc. Money! Everyone loves it, but few hold it in proper perspective. Let's be sure the previous statement does not apply to us.

More wars and arguments have been fought over this one thing than almost any other (Except the whole toilet seat affair). In this section we will begin by addressing the same points which have permeated this entire book. Those points will be money in regards to; the "one flesh principle," Agape love, open communication, and common sense.

Who does it belong to?

So numerous are the misconceptions of family finance, I struggled in determining where to start. Although many couples I counsel do not openly talk with me about money, I typically sense that it is, "the elephant in the room." Whenever this is the case, I attempt to gradually "pick" them for information on their feelings about the matter. Usually, within seconds, the conversation hits a dead end at one particular juncture. The juncture of who controls the money. I will beg your pardon for oversimplification here, but the truth is just that, simple. Every penny that becomes the possession of a Christian belongs to God. Therefore, He should be the one who controls it. I told you it was an easily understood premise. Easily said maybe, but admittedly, not so easily done. First, let me amply prove the point of ownership before proceeding.

"Every good gift and every perfect gift is from above, and cometh down from the Father of lights, with whom is no variableness, neither shadow of turning." James 1:17

" Ask, and it shall be given you; seek, and ye shall find; knock, and it shall be opened unto you: 8 For every one that asketh receiveth; and he that seeketh findeth; and to him that knocketh it shall be opened. 9 Or what man is there of you, whom if his son ask bread, will he give him a stone? 10 Or if he ask a fish, will he give him a serpent? 11 If ye then, being evil, know how to give good gifts unto your children, how much more shall your Father which is in heaven give good things to them that ask him?" Matthew 7:7-11

"The earth is the Lord's, and the fullness thereof; the world, and they that dwell therein." Psalm 24:1

"For every beast of the forest is mine, and the cattle upon a thousand hills. *11* I know all the fowls of the mountains: and the wild beasts of the field are mine." Psalm 50:10-11

Basketball great, Larry Bird was once quoted as saying, "I really don't like talking about money. All I can say is that the Good Lord must have wanted me to have it."   I could easily say the opposite, as I have very little money. I do however, understand and agree with Larry. Whatever I have, came from, and still belongs to, God.   Scripture clearly teaches this fact, and further instructs us, to seek His counsel in how to be good stewards of all of our resources **(Ref. 1 Corinthians 4:2, Luke 12:42, Proverbs 3:5-7).** Many times, instead of viewing money in this light, we are prone to take culture's selfish stance. The old saying, "What's mine is mine and what's yours is mine," manifests itself in marriage too often. This line of thought is detrimental to all marriages, and downright wrong in that of Christians. How could this possibly fit into the "one flesh" principle? How does this line of thinking fit into the definition of selfless agape love? It does not.

Hindrances to Proper Understanding

I have not been living with my head in the sand, therefore am not unaware of the complexity of this issue. I fully understand there are many hindrances to this being implemented in marriages. These hindrances may include, but certainly are not limited to; mistrust, past mismanagement, unnecessary debt, and plain old selfishness. These issues are very real, and must be factored into the final solution. Logically though, they do not offer exclusion from God's guidelines. Remember, we act upon God's will because He says so, and because we love and trust Him. If we allow extenuating circumstances to keep us from doing His will, then we are either displaying or fostering a lack of love and trust in Him. This being said, here are some general guidelines in regards to finance in the Christian marriage.

Communication

Money is no exception to the *good* communication principles, previously discussed at length. Even in cases where money has been a sore spot, or completely mismanaged, there is hope. This hope begins with communicating your true feelings about your finances. Once you have both had this opportunity, you should then devise a plan together on how to proceed. I must caution you, this will not produce anything beneficial unless you use the Biblical guidelines for good communication. If, however, you care enough about doing this God's way, and communicate effectively, seemingly insurmountable problems **can** be solved.

Common Wealth

When I reach this point of the seminar, I usually get "turned off" by many participants. This is precisely why I do not include a notes page in the workbook that accompanies the study. I figure if they aren't going to listen, they will have to find somewhere else to practice their doodling skills. My heartfelt opinion is that I am ignored in this regard due to the extreme discomfort the truth generates. Coupled with this, is the extreme trust that has to be implemented for success. In hopes that you will not "turn me off" by skipping this portion, I will proceed. Having established the Supreme ownership of the money we share, we must also establish the earthly partnership of the money. Without dragging this out unnecessarily, ponder these points, and what your correct reaction towards them should be;

- If you and your spouse are considered "one flesh", then doesn't it stand to reason that all money belongs to the partnership? **(Genesis 2:24)**
- If agape love mandates selflessness, shouldn't selfishness be exterminated in regards to our money as well? **(1 Corinthians 13:5)**
- If honesty is a Christian virtue, do we not have an obligation to our spouse to be forthright in money matters? **(Exodus 20, Ephesians 4)**

If you are feeling a bit of discomfort at this point, know you are not alone. Do not, however, allow discomfort to rob you of the blessings God has in store for obedience. If you truly are a Christian, then you trust God. You know that His way is perfect **(Ref. Psalm 18:30).** You are aware that his word cannot lie **(Ref. Titus 1:2)**. It's time to, "put your money where your mouth is!" These principles may not make you rich this side of glory, but the return on your investments of obedience, are out of this world.

Do not be misled into thinking that this chapter contains sufficient guidelines for all money matters within the Christian home. The author encourages you to seek further counsel from God's word, and those financial counselors who rely upon it.

Understanding the truth of the proverb telling us laughter is good medicine, I just had to share this bit of humor:

Who was the greatest financier in the Bible? Noah of course, he floated his stock, while the rest of the world was in liquidation!

Chapter Ten

"Bull's-eye"

"You'll shoot your eye out!" These are the infamous words that serve as the recurring motif in the classic holiday film, *A Christmas Story*. Rarely does a Christmas come and go without my family seeing this comedy at least twice. This is one of those things I could certainly live without, but not my wife. I would dare say this is her favorite holiday special. She especially enjoys the part where one of the main characters manages to get his tongue frozen to the flagpole.

I have a feeling she will enjoy it even more when we see this part in the coming year. I have this feeling because as she was dipping herself a bowl of ice cream just the other day, she made the mistake of licking the metal ice cream scoop. You guessed it, the scoop won this fight and took a piece of her lip as a trophy. My only regret is that I was not there to see my beautiful wife with an ice cream scoop hanging from her lip. If you recall my earlier story involving me and the superglue, you are probably thinking we are not the brightest bulbs on the tree. This is not true, we just live our lives at such a fast pace, we sometimes think as we are acting instead of before.

Okay, that story had absolutely nothing to do with my point, I just couldn't resist. Let's get back to the movie, and its correlation to this section of the book. Since there is a slight chance there is someone out there who has not seen the movie, I will give you a quick synopsis. The main character is a young man who desperately wants a BB gun for Christmas. Throughout the movie he is haunted by the words, "you'll shoot your eye out." He hears this daunting phrase from his parents, friends, teachers and even "Santa" at the mall. He makes every attempt to convince those around him this is not true. He assures them he will be careful and hit only what he aims at.

When I was about ten years old, I remember hearing those same dreadful words. My Uncle Larry and Aunt Sandra had gotten me a brand new Red Bear bow. I was elated. This was my first real bow and arrow set. Prior to receiving this magnificent piece of fiberglass I had several tree branches strung with tobacco twine fashioned into a bow, but nothing like this beauty. This bow was candy-apple red, and had a real nylon string. Although I cannot remember for sure, I am almost certain I slept with it beside my bed for several months. Needless to say, I loved the gift. I couldn't wait to get home in the afternoons so I could run to the shed, grab my trusty weapon, and practice until I was made to come in for dinner. One Saturday my parents took me to visit my Grandparents at their lake house. Of course I took the bow along. Normally, all I wanted to do was get my bathing suit on and go for a swim, but not this time. I quickly set my target up against a pine tree, and began to display my archery skills for my Granddad. Suddenly, those words rang through the air drowning out everything around including the radio play-ing on the porch. "You'll shoot your eye out!" I lowered my bow and turned to see my Uncle Carter whom the kids all loved because he enjoyed picking on us. I knew he was just aggravating me, but I felt a sudden urge to prove him wrong anyway. I pulled my straightest arrow out of the quiver, placed it carefully on the string, calmly pulled it back into firing position and concentrated on the very center of the target. Bull's-eye! The arrow had sailed off the string and landed dead center of the mark. I am not sure if my Grandfather or Uncle even saw it, but I did. Mission accomplished. I had hit the mark, and didn't even come close to my eye!

If you are wondering where in the world I am heading with this, I will finally tell you. Just as I had a strong desire to "hit the mark" with my arrow, I believe every true Christian desires to do the same in regards to parenting. No one would tell you that they wanted to be a mediocre Father or Mother. Every sincere believer wants to "hit the mark" when it comes to being a good parent. I certainly do not desire to miss the mark on something so important, because I realize I am raising someone's future spouse. Even more important is the immense responsibility of raising one of the next participants in God's great plan. I shudder to think my failure at this task could result in a lousy spouse, or leech on society. My hearts desire is to raise the kind of individual I would like to have as a partner in life. Someone who will seek to employ the principles found in this book, and more importantly God's word in an effort to be the best they can be for their husband/wife. I desire to rear an individual who is a productive part of society as he follows God. I want to hit the bull's-eye!

As you have probably noticed I spent a great deal of time using shooting and arrow metaphors in my introduction. This was not just an attempt to tell a couple of funny stories, it was by design. God Himself was the first to use such word play, as He spoke through Solomon in **Psalm 127**.

"Children are a heritage of the Lord: and the fruit of the womb is his reward. 4 As arrows are in the hand of a mighty man; so are children of the youth. 5 Happy is the man that hath his quiver full of them: they shall not be ashamed." Psalm 127:3-5

Solomon used the imagery of weapons pointing to children as those who could help defend the family. He is also attempting to bring out the immense blessing children can be. To further help us see the beauty of children, let's take a moment to view a similar passage from King Solomon as a doting Grandfather.

"Children's children are the crown of old men; and the glory of children are their fathers." Proverbs 17:6

Wait, did you catch the last part of that verse? Initially we see what we already know, that grandchildren are precious. In the final words however, we see there is an exhortation for Father's to be the glory of their children. The inference here is simple. The only time a child can truly have Godly pride in his Father is when the Father hits the mark! The mark God Himself has prescribed. This holds true with Mothers also **(Ref. Proverbs 31:28)**.

Understanding there is no way to adequately cover all topics of hitting this mark in Godly parenting, our goal will be more specialized. We will focus on the primary goal of parenting, followed by some very basic principles in accomplishing this goal.

Within the scope of Christian parenting lies the ultimate goal of training the child in the ways of God.

"Train up a child in the way he should go: and when he is old, he will not depart from it." Proverbs 22:6

"And, ye fathers, provoke not your children to wrath: but bring them up in the nurture and admonition of the Lord." Ephesians 6:4

When my wife and I were in the initial stages of our relationship, my ignorance caused us to have an uncomfortable discussion. As we were discussing the future and how we felt about numerous issues, the subject of children entered the conversation. I confessed I felt ill-equipped to be a good parent, but knew God would direct me when the time came. Melissa quickly attempted to admonish me with scripture as she often does. The encouragement she offered was the very passage I just quoted from **Proverbs 22**. Something just didn't sound right to me when she indicated that I should train my future children. I thought for a brief second and quipped, "I intend to raise my children, training is for animals!" In her usual gracious way, Melissa said, "but I thought you said you wanted to do it God's way." She then encouraged me to read **Proverbs 22** for myself. Sensing I had just opened my mouth and inserted both feet, I let it drop. Later that evening I went home and read the passage she had suggested. After spending a great deal of time determining the difference between training and raising children, I begged God's pardon, and thanked him for this new found knowledge.

What I found through this time of study was profound. To raise something is simply to make it grow. Raising something is just a matter of providing the necessities of life, at the right times. Even my five year old has great success in raising things. Just last year he grew the finest Chia pet you've ever seen. I doubt very seriously anyone would trust him to train something though. To train is; to direct the development of something, to instruct or prepare, to aim. Training is something that takes great time and effort, with the end goal of aiming the child in the right direction-just like an arrow bound for the mark. Hopefully you see the extreme difference in the two terms as I did. In the spiritual sense I see my responsibility to feed my children the "pure milk of the word" and thereby watch them grow.

"As newborn babes, desire the sincere milk of the word, that ye may grow thereby." 1 Peter 2:2

In the general sense however, my goal in parenting is not to simply feed a child and watch them grow. My goal is to bring a child up in such a way that they could easily reach the center of God's will for their lives. I assume you share this goal, for it is the mark prescribed in scripture.

We will now work forward on my prior assumption that you desire to train your children in the way they should go. Parenting is a complicated and difficult process to many Christians because they themselves often find they have not been "trained well enough in the way they should go." The sad truth is many adult Christians are still spiritual "babes on the bottle." Due to a lack of discipleship on the part of many churches, and their own parents, spiritually immature adults find themselves entrusting the training of their children to people outside the home. This practice is becoming more common in today's society and is leading to a further spiritual breakdown in general. I cannot stress enough the importance of training your children yourself. God entrusted them to you, and expects you to be their primary source of spiritual training. This is not to imply churches, daycares and others should be excluded entirely. I am a firm believer in giving the "entire village" a part in raising well-rounded children. I am also a firm believer this should not take place at the expense of the parent's Godly responsibility. This entire tangent is to reach one point. The point is, a child should be trained according to the instructions God gave us for life. This instruction manual is called the Bible. Within this manual answers and guidance to all parenting questions may be found.

"All scripture is given by inspiration of God, and is profitable for doctrine, for reproof, for correction, for instruction in righteousness." 2 Timothy 3:16

Proper training of children cannot occur unless one knows and applies the instructions in their own lives.

"Study to show thyself approved unto God, a workman that needeth not to be ashamed, rightly dividing the word of truth." 2 Timothy 2:15

I completely understand the temptation to avoid using directions. I am a typical male who used to discard the instructions before beginning a project. After numerous incidents of remaining parts and ruined purchases, I have become a believer in the directions. Where your children are concerned, I hope you will share this philosophy.

Having discussed the goal, and the means to reach it, let's look briefly at three major points.

Godly Roles

Often in homes today scriptural roles are overlooked. In many cases the children are ruling their homes, in direct violation of God's plan.

"Children, obey your parents in the Lord: for this is right." Ephesians 6:1

"Children, obey your parents in all things: for this is well pleasing unto the Lord." Colossians 3:20

When children are given no clear boundaries they take complete control. Parents must steer away from their innate desire to be "the good guy" and accept their parental responsibility to be leaders of the Christian home. Aside from this being scripturally wrong, the risk of damaging the marriage itself increases drastically. If life in the home revolves entirely around the children, consider where the marriage is left when the children are grown and gone. Whether you have children or contemplate having them, remember your spouse came first. You must never lose sight of the fact that you and your spouse are one flesh. Children should be incorporated into your life as one, not wedged between (See figure 5). I am frequently visited

> *Bring a child up in such a way*
>
> *that they can easily reach*
>
> *the center of God's will*
>
> *for their lives.*
>
> ∽◌⊙◌∽

by parents who have recently become "empty-nesters" as their children have left for school or some other endeavor. Although they miss the children greatly, their biggest problem is getting to know their spouse again. After a couple of decades of focusing on their kids, they realize they're living with a total stranger. Nowhere in scripture are parenting responsibilities given precedence over marital responsibilities. Ladies should continually remind themselves of the love that drew them to their "prince-charming". Husbands should be ever mindful of the love that drew them to their "queen". In short, you be the parent and don't forget your Godly role as a spouse in the process.

Team Effort

In regards to parenting, do not forget the "one flesh" principle of marriage which I have offered in abundance. You and your spouse are to be a team in every endeavor. Parenting is certainly no exception to the necessity of teamwork. Do not buy into culture's unfounded stereotypes in matters of parenting. Developing a child's heart and character is a big job. A job never intended for a single parent. If you are the Dad who leaves the "training" to your wife, you are not fulfilling your responsibility to God as it concerns your child. Perhaps you are the Mom who expects Dad to perform all of the disciplinary functions within the home, you are equally missing the mark. I have yet to find a single scripture that insinuates parenting is anything less than a joint effort. You and your spouse must work together in this effort to be most effective. Every facet of life within the home should display solidarity, and Godliness. This is crucial since your children will inevitably emulate what they see in you. Never act/react in any way you would not want your kids to mimic.

Always remember you were an equal partner in creating the precious life of your child, and you are to be an equal partner in nurturing this life.

If by chance you are one who has to travel this parenting road alone, let me pause to encourage you. Although God intended parenting to be a team effort, He can and will increase your ability and strength to do this alone, as you seek Him.

"I can do all things through Christ which strengtheneth me." Philippians 4:13

"But seek ye first the kingdom of God, and His righteousness; and all these things shall be added unto you." Matthew 6:33

Each Child An Individual

Before we close this chapter, let's take time to reflect on one last point of parenting. In God's magnificent plan, each individual life was created and gifted to fulfill certain roles. **(Ref. Ephesians 4:11-16)** Many parents forget this premise, and attempt to create carbon copies of themselves in their offspring. Parenting is not a "cookie-cutter process." With a watchful eye, encourage your children to become exactly who God created them to be. As you attempt to train your children in the way they should go, remind them often to listen for the Spirit. As they grow in the admonition of the Lord, they will begin to see the direction He is taking them in life. Whatever this direction is, (assuming it lines up with scripture) encourage it. Living vicariously through your children may hamper their effectiveness where it relates to their God-ordained purpose.

As summary for this brief segment on parenting I will leave you with this: We are not the Grand Architect of our children's lives, just God's contractor. Be certain you proceed according to His specifications. The result will be a direct hit – bull's-eye!

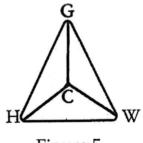

Figure 5

Chapter Eleven

"The One Another's of Marriage"

For the next two chapters I will offer you some good practices in marriage followed by bad practices. In reality, these are the same principles we have already discussed in previous discussions within the book. Since I am a firm believer in repetition as a learning tool, I have compiled these ideas into a more user-friendly format. In order to make these principles more useful as tools in your marriage I will employ a listing technique. Having these practices in list form should lend itself to book marking the pages for ease of future reference. I cannot encourage you enough to do just that, mark the proceeding lists and refer back to them often. I would especially encourage this practice in regard to the list of "one another's" found on the next couple of pages. I must pause for a moment to thank Dr. Howard Eyrich for his inspiration in the forming of this list, which will improve the satisfaction level in any marriage. Beyond improving the human satisfaction level in your marriage, I am thoroughly convinced these "one another's" will improve God's satisfaction level in your marriage. To a true Christian His satisfaction level is paramount. So let's dive right in.

- ## Acceptance of one another

Realize and accept imperfection. You did not marry perfection, therefore must not expect it. *"We then that are strong ought to bear the infirmities of the weak, and not to please ourselves. 2 Let every one of us please his neighbour for his good to edification. 3 For even Christ pleased not Himself; but, as it is written, The reproaches of them that reproached thee fell on Me. 4 For whatsoever things were written aforetime were written for our learning, that we through patience and comfort of the scriptures might have hope.5 Now the God of patience and consolation grant you to be likeminded one toward another according to Christ Jesus: 6 That ye may with one mind and one mouth glorify God, even the Father of our Lord Jesus Christ.7 Wherefore receive ye one another, as Christ also received us to the glory of God. Romans15:1-7*

- ## Admonish one another

Daily encourage growth and discourage sin in the home. *"And I myself also am persuaded of you, my brethren, that ye also are full of goodness, filled with all knowledge, able also to admonish one another." Romans 15:14*

- **Serve one another**

Sacrifice and work for the good of the other always. *"For, brethren, ye have been called unto liberty; only use not liberty for an occasion to the flesh, but by love serve one another." Galatians 5:13*

- **Bear with one another**

Be ever mindful that all differences may not be sin. Within this realm do not make mountains of mole hills. Practice patience on a regular basis. *"Put on therefore, as the elect of God, holy and beloved, bowels of mercies, kindness, humbleness of mind, meekness, longsuffering; 13 Forbearing one another, and forgiving one another, if any man have a quarrel against any: even as Christ forgave you, so also do ye. 14 And above all these things put on charity, which is the bond of perfectness. 15 And let the peace of God rule in your hearts, to the which also ye are called in one body; and be ye thankful. 16 Let the word of Christ dwell in you richly in all wis-*

dom; teaching and admonishing one another..." Colossians 3:12-16a

(Further Ref. Philippians 4:11, 2 Peter 1:5-8)

- **Be honest with one another**

Never forget truth is a mandate for the Christian and the Christian's marriage. Secrets are destructive and unacceptable. *"Lying lips are abomination to the Lord: but they that deal truly are His delight. " Proverbs 12:2*

- **Be tender-hearted with one another**

Gentleness is a fruit of the Spirit, which must be present in the home. Take care to consider your actions and spouse's reactions before proceeding in any given situation. Mingle compassion and humility into your actions. *"But the fruit of the Spirit is love, joy, peace, longsuffering, gentleness, goodness, faith, 23 Meekness, temperance: against such there is no law." Galatians 5:22-23 ;"Put on therefore, as the elect of God, holy and beloved, bowels of mercies, kindness, humbleness of mind, meekness, longsuffering."*

Colossians 3:12 (**Further Ref. Ephesians 4:32, 1 Peter 3:8**)

- **Forgive one another**

True forgiveness is mandatory in the Christian walk. Never resurrect past mistakes and use as ammunition, forgive and forget. Remember the forgiveness we were given and return as "little Christ's." *"Forbearing one another, and forgiving one another, if any man have a quarrel against any: even as Christ forgave you, so also do ye." Colossians 3:13* (**Further Ref. Ephesians 4:3, Jude 1:22**) Offering true forgiveness will benefit you as well. Failure to forgive is as foolish as holding a lit firecracker in your hand. You are the one who will be hurt most. Get rid of the firecracker and enjoy the release.

** *Forgiveness is the fragrance the violet sheds on the foot of the one who crushes it.* -Mark Twain

- **Comfort one another**

Life is difficult at times, encourage and comfort your mate when they are hurting. *"Rejoice with them that do rejoice, and weep with them that weep. Romans 12:13* (**Further

Ref. Galatians 6:1-4, 1 Thessalonians 4:18, Colossians 4:6)

- **Be devoted to one another**

Commitment is crucial through thick and thin, be mindful of the vows you made before God and man. ("For better or worse, in sickness, and in health, etc.") *"Fulfill ye My joy, that ye be likeminded, having the same love, being of one accord, of one mind. 3 Let nothing be done through strife or vainglory; but in lowliness of mind let each esteem other better than themselves." Philippians 2 "Be kindly affectioned one to another with brotherly love; in honour preferring one another." Romans 12:10*

It does not take a professional counselor to realize this list of "one another's" will prove useful in marriage. It does however, take a burning desire, discipline, and practice. There is no question this will require a lot of work. The good news is, just like most other disciplines the results will be well worth the effort. I can also tell you from personal experience, these practices become addictive, and even contagious.

In closing let me share with you one last "one another" for the list, which aptly summarizes the rest. LOVE ONE ANOTHER! Not just any love will do here, be sure it is agape love. **(Ref. 1 Corinthians 13)** Never forget that love, above all, is the gift of one's self! Daily seek to give the gift of yourself to the one who has made you complete in the spiritual sense (God), as well as the one He used to make you complete in the human sense (Your spouse).

Chapter Twelve

"Don't You Dare"

After spending three wonderful nights presenting the material found within the pages of this book, I wrapped up the final meeting of this particular seminar with an altar call. The call was to come forward if you truly desired God's blessings on your marriage. This call held the caveat that you must be willing to make the necessary commitments to make these blessings possible. I was ecstatic as I watched almost every couple in the congregation kneel on that altar and pray beside their spouse. After this time of worship and dedication, we prayed corporately, and began to dismiss. Within about thirty minutes everyone had said their good-byes and only a handful of people remained. As my family and I were packing up to leave, the Pastor of the church ran in and told me I was needed outside. I quickly headed out the door to see what was going on. When I got outside I found a young lady, who had left some time earlier, sitting in her vehicle sobbing. I was about to ask her what the trouble was, when I realized she was alone. This would not have been unusual had she left alone, but I knew better. When she left the seminar her husband was with her. After sorting through the tears and broken words I was able to gather that her husband had gotten out of the car and was walking somewhere between the church and home. Upon leaving the seminar they had begun to discuss many of the things I taught. Sadly, they had also begun to practice some of the things I had presented. The results were disastrous.

At this point you may be thinking to yourself, if this is what your teaching avails, I don't need it. Before passing that judgment, let me finish the story. The material within this book was designed to shed light on areas of discomfort and potential trouble within marriage. When presented it does just that. Once the information enlightened this particular couple to some of their current issues, they decided to act upon these issues quickly. This is the goal, illumination and proper reaction to it. So what went wrong? That is the question I needed an answer to, and found quite easy to come by.

After jumping into our Jeep and riding for about twenty minutes I found the young man on the side of the road, still making his unplanned trek towards home. I opened the door and he gladly accepted the invitation to get into a warm vehicle. I immediately turned around and headed back to the church where his lovely bride was waiting. On the return trip all I needed to know was one thing, was this young man willing to sit and talk in an attempt to work this out. Not only was he willing, he could hardly wait. His heart, like that of his mate, was breaking. This couple truly wanted to make things better, and was bewildered by what had happened.

When we arrived back at the church, I asked the Pastor for a quiet place to meet, which he gladly provided. The couple followed me in, sat down beside each other, and immediately began to apologize to one another. All of this took place without any prompting. What a great start.

Over the next hour we sat and talked through exactly what had happened. It was easy to see they were genuinely attempting to make the improvements discussed in the seminar. I also quickly discovered what had gone wrong. Although they were trying to do the right things, human nature reared its ugly head and caused them to do the opposite. Stay tuned for the end of this story, which I will present in a moment. For now, we will go another direction.

What I will share with you for the bulk of this chapter is a list of ten sure-fire ways to make a problem worse. In our discussions, the couple and I determined they had employed all ten of these "Don't You Dares". Why do I share such a story? To offer you another guarantee: Although I am confident in the power of the principles in this work, and their ability to make marriages stronger, I am also keenly aware of human nature. Human nature will enter the picture when we least expect it and cause us to stray from the principles of God. When this happens problems will arise. When these problems arise, I guarantee the following ten practices will make the problem worse!

• **Outbursts of anger** – This will effectively tear down your spouse, and home. Keep in mind, *"...the wrath of man worketh not the righteousness of God." James 1:20*

• **Manipulation** - This would entail turning the argument around to make yourself the victim, even when you know better. *"Judge not, that ye be not judged. 2 For with what judgment ye judge, ye shall be judged: and with what measure ye mete, it shall be measured to you again. 3 And why beholdest thou the mote that is in thy brother's eye, but considerest not the beam that is in thine own eye? 4 Or how wilt thou say to thy brother, Let me pull out the mote out of thine eye; and, behold, a beam is in thine own eye? 5 Thou hypocrite, first cast out the beam out of thine own eye; and then shalt thou see clearly to cast out the mote out of thy brother's eye." Matthew 7:1-5*

This could also be manifested in attempting to get your way even when it is totally contrary to your mate's. This is <u>not</u> agape love.

• **Silence** - Remember our spiel on communication? Silence is not *good* communication. **(Ref. Chapters 6 & 7)**

• **Ignoring problems** - This only causes problems to grow/become ammunition for future disagreements. Deal with all problems quickly, *"...let not the sun go down upon your wrath." Ephesians 4:26b*

• **Sulking** - Neither you or your spouse are children, therefore you must depart from childish ways. *"When I was a child, I spake as a child, I understood as a child, I thought as a child: but when I became a man, I put away childish things." 1 Corinthians 13:11*

•**Provocation** – the only provocation that is acceptable in marriage is that unto love. *"And let us consider one another to provoke unto love and to good works." Hebrews 10:24.*

Provocation is terribly destructive, *"But if ye bite and devour one another, take heed that ye be not consumed one of another." Galatians 5:15*

• **Deception** - Deception is a practice of the Devil, do not join forces with him against your spouse. *"Lie not one to another, seeing that ye have put off the old man with his deeds." Colossians 3:9*

• **Harsh Words -** This is clearly unacceptable Christian communication, which has no place in the home. *"With all lowliness and meekness, with longsuffering, forbearing one another in love." Ephesians 4:2*

• **Sarcasm** – Sarcasm's only acceptable place is in humor. This is no more than a veiled form of communicating derogatory remarks. *"Speak not evil one of another, brethren." James 4:11*

Holding Grudges - This is a failure to live out the necessary forgiveness of the Christian walk. Grudges drive wedges in the hearts of both participants. *"Grudge not one against another, brethren, lest ye be condemned: behold, the judge standeth before the door." James 5*

Be ever mindful of the immense forgiveness given to you by Christ, this is your example.

As we bring this chapter to a close, let me just make one concise point. I did not share these items in order for you to practice them.

I am firm believer however, we must be aware of the enemy's tactics if we are to overcome them. I cannot caution you enough here, do not be tempted to prove/disprove my guarantee. Take it from me, as well as the couple I mentioned earlier in the chapter. We can assure you, these things **will** make problems worse. On the same token, I did not offer this list as ammunition against your spouse. Do not pull this book out and wield it against your partner to show them where they are failing in this regard. Instead, use it to identify where *you* are failing. Highlight the areas that plague you most and then pray for help in their defeat. With a little practice and a lot of grace, you can stop these destructive practices. When you accomplish this, you will be amazed at the effectiveness of *good* problem solving. (Notice I said *good* problem solving. In this chapter I have shared what we should not be doing. Join me in the next to discover what we should be doing.)

As promised, here is the rest of the story we began earlier. I am happy to leave you with good news. The couple I shared about is doing great. May your story be a "happily ever after" too. When problems arise, and you begin to drift into the practices above, hear the voice of reason, **"Don't You Dare!"**

Chapter Thirteen

"You Got the Right One Baby"

I have always been amazed at how good most advertising agencies are at what they do. I often catch myself humming a tune from some cheesy commercial for a product I never even heard of. It seems that when this happens, it takes days for me to get the tune out of my head. Most of you will recall the campaign launched by one of the "cola giants" some years ago starring the legendary Ray Charles. There he sat at his beautiful baby grand, singing his heart out with that familiar red, white and blue can on top of the piano. By now you may already be singing the tune, "you got the right one baby…." I cannot tell you how many times that catchy little jingle has been in perpetual replay mode in my mind. I'll bet many of you reading this book now have the tune stuck in your head as well. Sorry.

Whoever wrote that particular tune truly did their job well. The point of their work is to somehow make you remember their product. Though the use of repetition, habit forming tunes and "eye candy," they are often effective in making their product seem better than the rest.

In this chapter, I hope that by attaching a well-known catch phrase to the title, and via repetition, you will remember the main point. My goal is to help you understand that although I am not peddling a product, I am offering a truth that is far superior to any other.   The truth I offer is how to better solve marriage problems when they arise.

In the first seminar I ever did I was asked, "Why did you have a list of ten things on how to make a problem worse, and only one thing on how to make a problem better?" I perceived this to be a fair question so I answered as such, "Because this one thing is more powerful than all ten things in the "don't you dare" list combined!" I am convinced you will agree.

The truth I am building towards is this: DWJD. There you have it, now get out there and do it.   Oh wait, I did not explain what DWJD was, did I? In the nineties a Christian slogan hit the scene, and took the country by storm. Everywhere you looked people were wearing brightly colored bracelets with the inscription WWJD. My bracelet was dark blue, and I wore it proudly everywhere I went. Soon the slogan was plastered on car bumpers, billboards, and even t-shirts. I realize very few people need to be reminded of the definition of WWJD, but for the sake of being thorough I will. The letters of WWJD represented the words, "What Would Jesus Do." What a wonderful way to be reminded of the correct way of making decisions. Surely, one donning such reminders would always stop to think about how Christ would react to a particular situation. I would like to think this was true, but even if it were, a crucial element was left out of the mix. Let me take a detour at this point to share another personal experience.

Before going into full-time ministry I worked in radiology at a hospital approximately thirty miles from my home. Each day I would make the drive alone on a relatively nice stretch of highway with all of the other commuters from my hometown. These other commuters were all clearly in a bigger hurry to get to work than I. The speed limit was posted as 55 miles per hour on this stretch of road, but my fellow travelers believed this to be merely a suggestion. I am not implying I never exceeded this speed limit in my four-teen years of travel, but I will say these folks made me look like I was in reverse most of the time. One particular spring morning I was traveling along in the right lane, when I noticed someone attempting to hook the front of their car onto my trailer hitch. I sped up just a bit to give us both some room, but apparently this was not enough. For about a mile I watched this NASCAR want-to-be use some very colorful language as they "drafted" off of my truck. I wish I thought they were attempting to conserve fuel, but this turned out not to be the case. When we finally hit an open stretch of highway and the driver was able to get into the passing lane, they made a move that would have made even Richard Petty envious. With one quick jerk the driver was able to whip their vehicle into the passing lane, blow by me, then slide back onto the road directly in front of me. What made this such an incredible piece of driving is the fact that they were able to do this with just one hand. That's right just one hand, because they were using the other to give me some sort of signal using their middle finger. Assuming they were wishing me a good day, I smiled and waved. To get to my point, there is one detail of the story left to share. Once this car passed me I was disheartened to see a Christian fish symbol with a WWJD sticker close beside on the car's bumper.

Here is my point, WWJD asks the question of what Jesus would do, but fails to assume application. In the same logic offered in the very beginning of this book, application must accompany knowledge for change to occur. It was not enough for this driver to <u>ask</u> what Jesus would do. They also had to <u>act</u> on what Jesus would do. Certainly He would not have acted in such a manner.

DWJD may help us complete the picture. Representing "Do What Jesus Did," let's apply this acronym to problem solving. In order to effectively solve marriage problems when they arise, we must search the scriptures for how Jesus would handle specific situations. Once we have found the answer we must then do something with it. Without doubt, life in modern times is much different than in the days when Jesus physically walked the earth. This fact however, does not lend credence to the thought process which would have us believe there is no way to know how Jesus would have reacted to particular situations today. As Solomon said in **Ecclesiastes 1:9**, there is nothing new under the sun.

"The thing that hath been, it is that which shall be; and that which is done is that which shall be done: and there is no new thing under the sun."

In other words, the details may change, but the basics remain the same. In almost thirty years of Bible study, I have yet to run across a problem that scripture does not deal with. I am doubtful to the point of complete certainty you will either. When we are truly seeking the answers to problems God is faithful to provide. When He does, we must then act on the provision.

In short, the vehicle to effective problem solving is emulation of Christ. Although this may sound too simple, there is no problem that cannot be solved by; asking ourselves how Christ would handle the issue, then following His example. After all, this is the definition of Christian; little Christ, or one who is like Christ.   When you get a firm grasp on these principles, and put them into action, "You Got the Right One Baby!"

"Be ye therefore followers of God, as dear children." Ephesians 5:1

"For even hereunto were ye called: because Christ also suffered for us, leaving us an example, that ye should follow His steps." 1 Peter 2:21

"Peace is not the absence of conflict, but the presence of God no matter what the conflict." – Author Unknown

Chapter Fourteen

Conclusion

I have often been told all good things must come to an end. I choose not to believe everything I hear. Although we are nearing the end of our time in this book together, the most important journey still lies ahead. This is not the end, rather it is a deep breath before a new beginning.

It seems as if there are so many things left unsaid, too many stones unturned, but at least I have been given the opportunity to share a piece of my heart with you, the reader. Although I genuinely appreciate you investing your time in this work, I hope the true beneficiary will be you. More than anything else my desire is to see marriages strengthened, love relearned, and joy fulfilled.

In our time together I hope you have gathered some useful tools and information to utilize within your marriage. Marriage is one of the most sacred institutions we have the privilege of participating in this side of glory. Join me in showing the world you believe this to be truth. It is an understatement to say that marriage is a lot like work, but by far worth the effort. The benefits of enjoying marriage

God's way far outweigh any energy you may expend in the process.

As you finish the words on these pages, take time to ponder all we have discussed. From identifying where we have missed the mark, to effective problem solving and everything in between, we have covered a lot of ground in a short time. Do not let the enemy lull you into feeling you have accomplished something by simply reading another marital improvement book. As I stated in my opening guarantee, knowledge must be accompanied by application for results to occur. Application is what I was referring to when I said the most important journey still laid ahead.

If you are that desperate soul who has read every work on the subject and tried all there is to try, yet still feel hopeless - snap out of it! Seize the moment right here, right now. In the words of my friend, brother and partner in ministry, Nicholas Perkins, "How could God not bless two individuals who are submissive to Christ and committed to Him as well as the covenant they made to Him?" The answer is simple, He cannot!   God's promise to bless those who seek Him cannot be broken. Integrity is part of who God is, not merely something He does.

Marriage, above all,

is a spiritual institution.

This means that with every step you take towards God's will in your marriage, blessings will follow. If you are a Christian you believe in the God of **Genesis 1:1** who had power to create the heavens and the earth. If this is accurate, believing He can and will bless your marriage as you follow His plan should be automatic. Begin right now discarding all of the lame excuses Satan will offer to keep you from applying these principles in your marriage. Here are a few of my favorites, accompanied by Biblical response;

I or my spouse just cannot change – untrue, only God is unchanging. *"Jesus Christ the same yesterday, and today, and forever." Hebrews 13:8, "Every good gift and every perfect gift is from above, and cometh down from the Father of lights, with whom is*

no variableness, neither shadow of turning."
James1:17

<u>I just can't do all of this</u> – true, you cannot, but God can through you as you yield your will to His. *"I can do all things through Christ which strengtheneth me." Philippians 4:13*

<u>We did not begin this way, it's just too late</u> – too late for what? It is never too late to follow God's path. *"If ye love Me, keep my commandments." John 14:15*. Did you see a time frame listed here? Neither did I. If you love Him, get to work.

<u>You left out too much, I need more to really fix things</u> – if you will not be faithful in a little, how can you be trusted with more? *"And he said unto him, Well, thou good servant: because thou hast been faithful in a very little, have thou authority over ten (more) cities." Luke 19:17* You are responsible to God for every piece of information you gather. Ignorance is no longer your defense

for any item found within the pages of this book.

<u>There's no way my husband/wife will do these things</u> – this is irrelevant.   **You** are responsible to God for doing what **you** know is right. *"So then every one of us shall give account of himself to God." Romans 14:12* Surely you do not believe that two people doing the wrong thing is appropriate.

In closing, allow me to share with you one final experience from my own personal souvenir collection. In February of 2002, Melissa and I traveled to York Harbor, Maine for some quality time together. When we arrived at the Bed & Breakfast we were awestruck with the beauty of our surroundings. After spending much of the day sightseeing, we settled in for some much needed rest. I will never forget the events of the next few minutes for as long as I live. Melissa has a great affinity for poetry and had sat by the fireplace to read some of her favorite selections. There we were sitting side by side in front of the crackling logs, watching snow fall onto the ocean outside our second story window. Suddenly, I realized how unworthy I was to be part of such a spiritual experience as marriage. At that very moment I felt my heart would beat out of my chest. Over the sounds of my racing heart, and waves crashing onto the cliffs outside, I heard my bride softly reciting the end of a timeless classic. These are the words from a Robert Browning prose I will forever remember…*"Come grow old with me, the best is yet to be."*

May God grant you the desire to whisper these same words to your spouse, and the strength to make it happen. May the best be yet to come for you and yours.

Pastor Dave

Chapter Fifteen

"A Marriage Prayer"

If you are one who genuinely desires to "do marriage" God's way, incorporate the following prayer into your personal quiet time. Your marriage deserves the best. God desires to deliver just that.

Almighty Father of light,

Illuminate my heart with truth from Your word,
Create in me an insatiable desire to act upon what I see.

Bless my marriage as I seek to display genuine love,
Restrain my heart when it deceives me, and leads me away from selflessness.

Grant me the ability to be the best I can be, for my spouse, but ultimately for You.

Accept my gratitude for giving me someone to share my heart with,
Give them the desire to share theirs as well.

Make me ever mindful of the enemy and his tactics,
Afford me the strength to stand against the world, and its faulty views.
Forgive me when I step away from your will, then quickly guide me back to You.

Assist me in making my home a dwelling place for Your loving Spirit,
Knowing that you alone can ensure, The Best is yet to Come.

                                        -Amen

Looking for a good marriage counselor?

I'm available!

-GOD

Appendix

The Best Is Yet To Come

Study Questions

Foundations

Before moving forward in this study we must understand one of the primary rules foundational to the Christian life in general, which applies to Christian Marriage as well.

1.) If we seek our comfort, fulfillment, pleasure and identity in any other source rather than _____ we are certain to be disappointed, and rob ourselves of the full joy that the Christian life has to offer.

2.) According to the Apostle Paul in 2 Corinthians 3:5, our sufficiency is found?

3.)   Our mates have the capacity to be everything we need and desire in life.
                    True   False

All In All

You are my strength when I am
weak
You are the treasure that I seek
You are my all in all
Seeking You as a precious jewel
Lord to give up, I'd be a fool,
You are my all in all
Jesus, Lamb of God, worthy is
Your name
Jesus, Lamb of God, worthy is
Your name
Taking my sin, my cross, my
shame
Rising again, I bless Your name
You are my all in all
When I fall down, You pick me
up
When I am dry, You fill my cup
You are my all in all.

©1999 Shepherd's Heart Music
Dennis Jernigan

Marriage is a Spiritual Institution

1.) Where in scripture do we find the first record of marriage?

2.) In order for marriage to be successful the betrothed must _____ all and _____ to one another. **(Ref. Genesis 2)**

3.) Although joined together in marriage both parties remain complete individuals in every sense of the word.   True   False

4.) Who gave the bride away in the first marriage ceremony?

What is Marriage?

Take time to jot down your own thoughts,
understandings and definitions of marriage and
what it should be.

_____

_____

_____

_____

_____

_____

_____

_____

_____

_____

_____

_____

_____

_____

_____

_____

_____

_____

_____

_____

Misconceptions

1.) Feelings are an adequate reasoning for getting married.   True   False

2.) Which of the following statements is most accurate? (hint: agape' love)

"Marriage is all about give and take."
"Marriage is all about give."

3.)   In marriage it is important to work through misconceptions by   _____
_____.

4.) How do we adjust expectations?

The Fix

1.) What "mayonnaise word" does the author claim as the fix for marital misconceptions?

2.) Define Superimposition as it pertains to this study.

3.) "We must stop imposing _____ ideas and expectations on our marriages, and begin superimposing _____ ideas and expectations on our marriages!"

Definitions and Absolutes

1.) What does Theo-Centric mean?

2.) How does this apply to marriage?

3.) Explain the premise behind **Ecclesiastes 4:10-12.**

_____

_____

_____

_____

_____

_____

_____

_____

Definitions and Absolutes
(Continued)

4.) Marriage is to be a picture of _____ and
_____ _____. **(Ref. Ephesians 5:22-31)**

5.) What was Christ's purpose toward His bride, the church? How does this apply to marriage?

6.) How is marriage similar to the Holy Trinity? Use illustrations to help prove your point.

7.) Marriage is a _____ effort since the two joined are now _____ _____.

Definitions and Absolutes
(Continued)

Take time to read through the passage below
which contains God's definition of love.
Highlight key terms in regards to true love and
pray for strength to display these traits in your
own life.

"Though I speak with the tongues of men
and of angels, and have not charity, I am
become as sounding brass, or a tinkling
cymbal. 2 And though I have the gift of
prophecy, and understand all mysteries, and
all knowledge; and though I have all faith, so
that I could remove mountains, and have not
charity, I am nothing. 3 And though I bestow
all my goods to feed the poor, and though I
give my body to be burned, and have not
charity, it profiteth me nothing.4 Charity
suffereth long, and is kind; charity envieth
not; charity vaunteth not itself, is not puffed
up, 5 Doth not behave itself unseemly,
seeketh not her own, is not easily provoked,
thinketh no evil; 6 Rejoiceth not in iniquity,
but rejoiceth in the truth; 7 Beareth all things,
believeth all things, hopeth all things,
endureth all things.

8 Charity never faileth: but whether there be prophecies, they shall fail; whether there be tongues, they shall cease; whether there be knowledge, it shall vanish away. *9* For we know in part, and we prophesy in part. *10* But when that which is perfect is come, then that which is in part shall be done away. *11* When I was a child, I spake as a child, I understood as a child, I thought as a child: but when I became a man, I put away childish things. *12* For now we see through a glass, darkly; but then face to face: now I know in part; but then shall I know even as also I am known. *13* And now abideth faith, hope, charity, these three; but the greatest of these is charity."

1 Corinthians 13:1-13

Hindrances to Effective Marriage

1.) What is Moral Relativism?

2.) How does Moral Relativism affect marriage today?

3.) We are commanded to be_____ the world, not _____ the world. Our thinking is to be radically different.

4.) Culture is fairly close to what is correct, we must simply modify its thought processes a little.

                    True   False

Hindrances to Effective Marriage (Continued)

5.)   One of the greatest hindrances to effective marriage is _____.

6.) Explore these thoughts on pride;

        Psalm 10:4   Proverbs 8:13
        Proverbs 11:2   Proverbs 13:10
        Proverbs 16:18 Romans 8:7-8

7.) How do we defeat this foe called pride? (Ref. Proverbs 3, Psalm 36, Psalm 51:10, & Proverbs 4:23-26)

Helps for Effective Marriage

1.) Good _____ is crucial in any successful relationship.

2.) List at least four characteristics of good communication.

_____

_____

_____

_____

_____

_____

3.) List at least four characteristics of poor communication.

_____

_____

_____

_____

_____

Helps for Effective Marriage
(Continued)

4.) The most important thing about physical relations in the marriage is personal pleasure.   True   False

5.) What is the real benefit of sex within the marriage?

6.) How does the principle of agape' love play into sexual relations within the marriage?

7.) What is God's pre-requisite for sexual intimacy?

8.) Explain how the "superimposition fix" applies to the physical aspect of marriage?

Helps for Effective Marriage
(Continued)

9.) Explain how the "one-flesh" principle applies to finances within the Christian home.

10.) Discuss three major aspects of God's view on money in the Christian marriage.

_____

_____

_____

_____

_____

_____

_____

_____

_____

_____

_____

Helps for Effective Marriage
(Continued)

11.) A child should always be the focus in the home?
   True   False

12.) Explain the importance of teamwork in parenting.

_____
_____
_____
_____
_____
_____

13.) We must remember that our children will _____ our actions and attitudes in life. Therefore, we must be careful to live Godly lives as they observe.

Helps for Effective Marriage
(Continued)

14.) Train your children via _____ not _____. **(Ref. Ephesians 6:4)**

15.) Raising and training are the same thing. True   False

16.) "We are not the Grand Architects in our children's lives' just the _____."

"One Anothers of Marriage"

Of the 10 "one anothers of marriage" covered by
the author within this book, list at least 5 along
with your understanding of them.

_____

_____

_____

_____

_____

_____

_____

_____

_____

_____

_____

_____

_____

_____

_____

_____

_____

_____

_____

How <u>Not</u> To Solve Marriage Problems

Within the body of this book 10 ways to make a problem worse are discussed. Take time to prayerfully consider the top 5 you know you may struggle with then list them below. Once you are done take time to pray for help in this regard daily.

_____

_____

_____

_____

_____

_____

_____

_____

_____

_____

_____

_____

_____

_____

_____

_____

_____

How <u>To</u> Solve Marriage Problems

Although you will be tempted to believe this is too simple to be effective, there is one simple solution that will solve <u>all</u> marriage problems. You did not misread, correctly applied the following will get you through any relational strife you may encounter.

_____ of Christ in fulfilling the picture of He and His bride will ensure that…

The Best Is Yet To Come !

"Come grow old with me, the best is yet to be."
- Robert Browning

Notes

Notes

Success Stories

If the material in this work has challenged, motivated, or otherwise touched your life in a positive way, the Author would love to hear about it. Take time to contact us to share your story. Rest-assured your anonymity will be protected unless you indicate otherwise!

ddcproductions@embarqmail.com

or

DDC 4 Him Productions
197 McIver Chambers Lane
Timberlake, NC 27583

GOD BLESS!

Seminar Invitation

If you are a Pastor or educator, and found the information within to be helpful, and are interested in having Pastor Chambers come to your facility to present a seminar series based on the book, please detach and mail the following to:

DDC 4 Him Productions
Ref. Best is Yet Seminar
197 McIver Chambers Lane
Timberlake, NC 27583

"4 HIM"

Yes,

I am interested in scheduling a seminar date with

Pastor Chambers, and may be reached at (   )

between the hours of _____ & _____. The

target audience for this seminar will be individuals

between the ages of _____ & _____.

_____
Contact Name

Also Available!

If you plan to use the information in this book for pre/post-marital counseling, you may wish to acquire the leader's guide and/or accompanying workbook for counselees available by mail order at:

DDC 4 Him Productions
Ref. Best is Yet Workbooks
197 McIver Chambers Lane
Timberlake, NC 27583

Or

Via the World Wide Web:
BestIsYet.net

I am interested in purchasing _____ Leader's
Guides at a cost of $4.00 each. _{Quantity}

I am interested in purchasing _____ workbooks
at a cost of $3.50 each. _{Quantity}

 Please ship booklets to the following address:

Name:_____
Address:_____
City, State, Zip_____
Phone /E-mail:_____

Coming Soon!

A new Devotional full of "Wonder Breaks" for Nature Lovers. Explore God's creation through the eyes of a small town Pastor as he shares inspirational devotions gathered from his favorite "thoughtful spot" the hammock!

"He hath made His wonderful works to be remembered: the LORD is gracious and full of compassion."
Psalm 111:4

CPSIA information can be obtained
at www.ICGtesting.com
Printed in the USA
FFOW02n0634230616
25293FF